Buddhist Philosophy and Culture

Quick and Concise

Buddhist Philosophy and Culture

Amar Bandyopadhyay

hachette INDIA

First published in 2025 by Hachette India
(Registered name: Hachette Book Publishing India Pvt. Ltd)
An Hachette UK company
www.hachetteindia.com

1

ISBN 978-93-5731-694-1

Hachette Book Publishing India Pvt. Ltd
4th & 5th Floors, Corporate Centre
Plot No. 94, Sector 44, Gurugram – 122003, India

Typeset in Athelas 11/15.4
by InoSoft Systems

Printed and bound in India
by Thomson Press India Ltd.

MIX
Paper | Supporting responsible forestry
FSC® C010615
www.fsc.org

CONTENTS

PREFACE

Before delving into this book, it is important to first clarify the meaning of the term 'Buddha' which is not a given name but a title. The word 'Buddha' comes from the Sanskrit root '*budh*' that means 'to awaken'. And therefore 'Buddha' is one who has awakened. The nature of a Buddha is a subject that the Buddhist tradition itself has expounded on at length and to which we will return below.

Since one 'becomes' a Buddha, and is not born as one, the title is bestowed upon enlightened beings, including figures from the Jataka tales. Exploring the key Buddhist concepts in *A Survey of Buddhism,* Bhikshu Sangharakshita says, 'The Buddhas are born not for themselves alone, but for the sake of all sentient beings, out of compassion for the world, for the welfare, profit and happiness of gods and men. They are world teachers and their teaching, though even the same, has to be discovered afresh by each of them before it can again be made known to the world.'

The *Bhagawad Purana*, the *Vishnu Purana*, and the *Garuda Purana* in Hindu mythology refer to Gautam Buddha as an incarnation of Lord Vishnu. However, traditional Buddhism does not recognize him as an all-powerful deity or a divine incarnation. As per the Buddhist perspective, Buddha as the Enlightened One was a historical figure. The prince of the Sakya clan, Siddharth Gautam renounced worldly pleasures and left his palace in search of truth. Upon attaining enlightenment after deep meditation, he discovered the truth about suffering and liberation. Thus he became the Buddha who is the founder of the Buddhist way of life. In this book, the term 'Buddha' primarily refers to Siddharth Gautam after his enlightenment.

The greatness of the Buddha lies not merely in his attainment of Nirvana, but in making that path attainable once more – not just for himself, but for countless millions across the ages.

Buddhist philosophy and doctrines based on the teachings of Gautama Buddha offer profound insights into reality and human existence. The central concern is to liberate individuals from suffering, attachment and ignorance, and provide the path to liberation. For the Buddha, the root cause of suffering is ignorance, and, in order to eliminate suffering, we need to know the nature of existence. Also, Buddha insisted that his doctrines must be accepted only after meeting all doubts and perplexities. Buddhism has all along recognized the distinction between relative and transcendental philosophy. This is the core of Buddhist philosophy.

Since Buddha's teachings were developed in the background of various ethical and religious notions, they did not come to us in a systematic form. In some chapters, therefore, we may come across overlapping ideas or repeated discussion of the four noble truths, the eightfold path, the doctrine of soul, and the controversies between the various Buddhist sects. Despite all this, the *sutras* which were held to be sacred by all the schools were retained.

Buddhism should be practised, not just studied. Its teachings are meant to be understood and applied. This book presents the key philosophical ideas of Buddhism in a simple and comprehensive manner. It aims to spark interest in Buddhist philosophy and serves as a valuable resource for students, especially those preparing for competitive exams.

I

WHO IS GAUTAM BUDDHA?

SOURCES OF INFORMATION

Siddhartha Gautama, known as the Buddha, is the founder of Buddhism. He is also referred to as Gotama Buddha, Gautama, or Gautam Buddha or Shakyamuni, meaning 'Sage of the Shakyas'. After attaining enlightenment, he was also called *Tathagata*. In Mahayana traditions, 'Shakyamuni' is used to distinguish the historical Buddha from other Buddhas mentioned in the *Sutras*. The name 'Buddha Shakyamuni' is also found in Ashoka's inscription at Lumbini.

As defined by Sir Monier Monier-Williams, Ernst Leumann, Carl Cappeller (2002) in the *Sanskrit–English Dictionary* – a couple of centuries after his death, he came to be known by the title Buddha, which means 'Awakened One' or 'Enlightened One'. Buddha, the'Awakened One' or the 'Enlightened One' is the masculine form of *budh*, which means 'to wake, be awake, observe, heed, attend, learn, become aware of, to know, be conscious again'. *Buddhi*, the power to 'form and retain concepts, reason, discern, judge, comprehend, understand' is the faculty which discerns *Satya* (truth) from falsehood.

Though it is confirmed that the Buddha is a historical figure, much of what is known about his life cannot be taken with absolute certainty. His traditionally accepted dates (566–486 BCE) remain approximate and are not definitively proven. The earliest scriptures do not provide a complete account of the Buddha's life. In fact, no Buddhist scripture contains a fully detailed biography. However, from the mid-3rd century BCE, several of Ashoka's edicts (268–232 BCE) mention the Buddha and Buddhism. For instance, in Minor Rock Edict No. 1, Ashoka refers to himself as a Buddhist *Upasaka* (lay follower) and a Buddha-Saka (follower of the Buddha). He also states that he has drawn closer to the *Sangha* and become more ardent in the faith (1-1). Particularly, Ashoka's Lumbini pillar inscription commemorates the emperor's pilgrimage to Lumbini, the recognized birthplace of the Buddha. In this inscription, the Buddha is referred to as the Buddha Shakyamuni, highlighting his identity as the sage of the Shakya clan. The name of his clan was Gautama (Pali: Gotama), meaning 'one who has the most light'. His given name Siddhartha means 'one who achieves his goal' (1-2).

In the time of the Buddha, Lumbini was situated east of Kapilavastu and south-west of Devadaha of Shakya, an oligarchic republic. According to the Buddhist tradition, this was the birthplace of the Buddha. The Ashoka Pillar of Lumbini, a monolithic column with an inscription in the ancient Brahmi script discovered at Rupandehi, in 1896, is believed to mark the spot of Ashoka's visit to Lumbini. The site was not known as Lumbini before the pillar was discovered (1-4).

According to the *Sutta Nipata*, the Buddha was born in a village of the Sakyans in the Lumbini Janapada. During his visit to Devadaha, he stayed in Lumbini Vana and preached the *Devadaha Sutta* (1-2).

Malalankara Watthu, a lesser-known but significant Sri Lankan text on Buddhist history and traditions, was found two thousand years after Buddha was born, and it was translated into English by Bigandet (1-3). In the *Jataka*, which contains the life stories of the Buddha, the preface narrates the first part of his life up to the age of 36. This text, in its commentarial form, was compiled around the fifteenth century CE (1-4). The Pali poem *Jina Carita* (The Conqueror's Career), written by Buddhadatta in the 13th century CE, narrates key episodes of the Buddha's life, covering events up to the age of 36 and the final few months of his life.

Another genre that emerged over time in various early Buddhist schools was the biography of the Buddha. Notable works in this genre include the *Mahavastu* of the Lokottaravada school, the *Lalitavistara Sutra* of the northern tradition, the *Theravada Nidanakatha,* and the *Dharmaguptaka Abhiniskramana Sutra* (1-3).

The *Mahavastu* (Great Story) is a canonical text of the Mahasaṃghika Lokottaravada school of early Buddhism. It is a composite collection of multiple life stories of Buddha Shakyamuni rather than a historical biography. It is a compilation of different texts by scholars compiled between two BCE–four CE.

The *Buddha Charitra* narrates the life of the Buddha, from his birth as Prince Siddhartha to his attainment of enlightenment. While the Chinese and Tibetan versions preserve the original epic with 28 cantos, the surviving Sanskrit text consists of only the first 18 cantos in their entirety, along with the first quarter of the 14th canto. These cantos cover the narrative up to the Buddha's victory over Mara, the lord of desire and illusion, symbolizing the triumph of wisdom and enlightenment over worldly temptations and delusions, and his enlightenment (1-5).

Buddhist poetry is a vast genre encompassing various styles and languages, including Sanskrit, Tibetan, Chinese, and Japanese. A notable Sanskrit Buddhist poet Matricheta composed devotional hymns in *sloka* form. In addition to the works of Asvaghosa and Matricheta, poetry in *sloka* form was also composed in regional Indian languages such as Tamil and Apabhramsha. One well-known example is the Tamil Buddhist epic *Manimekalai*, one of the five great epics of Tamil literature. Other later hagiographical Buddhist texts include the *Buddhavamsa*, the *Cariyapitaka*, and the *Vimanavatthu*.

Thus, we find fragmented biographical narratives of the Buddha's life. Though not entirely based on facts, these accounts remain valuable. While some narratives are partly fabricated or mythologised, they still hold significance. Despite contradictions, they cannot be dismissed. Historians have attempted to reconstruct a more accurate picture by combining early Buddhist sources, archaeological findings, and historical knowledge of the cultural and societal traditions of that era.

John Strong's *The Buddha: A Short Biography* is an excellent introduction to the Sanskrit and Pali narratives describing the Awakened One. The author introduces us to the key events in the life of the Buddha from his birth and enlightenment to the formation of the early Buddhist community, and his *parinirvana* (the end of the cycle of death and rebirth).

Prof. Rhys Davids rightly observed in his well-known book, *The History and Literature of Buddhism*, 'Clearly the only proper course to pursue is to go back behind these later poetical documents (Sir Edwin Arnold's *The Light of Asia*) to the actual text of the Three Pitakas themselves, to collect there whatever is said incidentally about the life, family, and personal surroundings of the Buddha, and to piece them together into a connected whole. This has not been done, and cannot of course be done in a satisfactory way until the whole of the text of the sacred canon shall have been published by the Pali Text Society or elsewhere.

Using common details from different sources, we can put together a basic account of his life. Today, the archaeological site of Tilaurakot in Nepal is believed to be the ancient Kapilavastu, the capital of the Shakya clan, and the birthplace of Gotama or Gautam Buddha. Again, the village and archaeological site of Piprahwa in Uttar Pradesh, India, just across the border from Nepal is also thought to be Kapilavastu. Both sites have significant evidence for their claims and recognition.

The archaeological sites of modern-day Piprahwa and Tilaurakot were first excavated in 1898–1899 CE by the British landowner William Claxton Peppe and then by the Indian archaeologist Purna Chandra Mukherjee between 1845–1903 CE. Since then, excavations have been ongoing periodically. Debate has been going on since that time regarding the importance of both the sites as Buddha's birth place and early years.

THE BIRTH OF GAUTAM BUDDHA

The ancient city of Kapilavastu was ruled by the oligarchy of the Shakya clan which maintained close ties to the nearby city of Devadaha which was controlled by the Koliyas. Both the clans claimed descent from the legendary Ikshvaku Dynasty.

From Buddhist texts, we come to know that Kapilavastu founded by King Ikshvaku and named after the great Sage Kapila whose philosophy (*Samkhya*) was honoured by the Shakya clan, was ruled by the Shakya chief Sihahanu, while the nearby city of Devadaha was ruled by his brother Anjana. The two cities maintained their alliance through intermarriage. Sihahanu's son Suddhodana was married to Anjana's daughter Maya.

After twenty childless years, one night, Maya dreamt that four divine spirits carried her away to a garden where they bathed, anointed, dressed her in white, and bestowed garlands of flowers upon her. Then, a white elephant appeared in the dream and circled her three times before entering her womb through the right side. Maya awoke the next morning knowing she was pregnant.

In due course, in keeping with tradition, she set out for Devadaha with her entourage. The group stopped at the gardens of Lumbini located between the two cities to rest. After her bath, Maya stepped from the pond and went into labour, giving birth to her son beneath a Sala tree, the branch of which she clung to for support. The newborn is said to have stood up as soon as he was born, took seven steps, and announced his arrival as a bringer of peace.

Rhys Davids wrote in *The Life of Buddha* – 'He was not born as ordinary men are; he descended of his own accord into his mother womb from his throne in heaven; he gave unmistakable signs, immediately after his birth, of his high character and of his future greatness. Earth and heaven united to pay him homage, the very tree bent on its own accord over his mother, and the angels and archangels were present with their help. His mother was the best and the purest of the daughters of men, and his father was of royal lineage, a king of wealth and power. It was a pious task to make his abnegation and his condescension greater by the comparison between the splendour of the position he was to abandon, and this poverty in which he afterwards lived. And in countries distant from Kapilavastu the inconsistencies between such glowing accounts, and the very names they contain passed unnoticed by credulous hearers' (1-3).

In this context, we may need to refer to another quote by Rhys Davids from the final volume of the *Journal of the Royal Asiatic Society.* This quote comes from the article *The Discourse on Wonders and Marvels* (*Acharya Abbhuta Sutta*) by Robert Chalmers. 'This is one of the dialogues referred to in the last Chapter 123 in the shorter collection. In it is laid down as true of each Buddha (and therefore also of the historical Buddha) that the universe is illumined with brilliant light at the moment of his conception; that the womb is transparent so that his mother can see the womb before it is born; that the pregnancy lasts exactly 280 days; that the mother stands during parturition; that on the birth of the babe it is received first into the hands of heavenly beings, and that supernatural showers provide first hot and then cold water in which the child is bathed; that the future Buddha walks and speaks at once, that the whole universe is again illumined with a brilliant light (1-6).'

Asvaghosa a renowned Indian Buddhist poet, philosopher, and scholar (1st–2nd century CE) mentions the same circumstances in *Buddhacharita,* an epic poem on the life of the Buddha (1-7).

'Having thus in due time issued from the womb, he shone as if he had come down from heaven, he who had not been born in the natural way, he who was born full of wisdom, not foolish, as if his mind had been purified by countless aeons of contemplation.

'With glory, fortitude, and beauty he shone like the young sun descended upon the earth; when he was gazed at, though of such surpassing brightness, he attracted all eyes like the moon.

'With the radiant splendour of his limbs, he extinguished like the sun the splendour of the lamps; with his beautiful hue as of precious gold he illuminated all the quarters of space.

'Unflurried, with the lotus-sign in high relief, far-striding, set down with a stamp – seven such firm footsteps did he then take – he who was like the constellation of the seven *Ṛṣis*.

'"I am born for supreme knowledge, for the welfare of the world – thus this is my last birth," thus did he of lion gait, gazing at the four quarters, utter a voice full of auspicious meaning.

'Two streams of water bursting from heaven, bright as the moon's rays, having the power of heat and cold, fell down upon that peerless one's benign head to give refreshment to his body.'

Another Buddhist source states that during King Sihahanu's reign, the country of Kapilavastu enjoyed peace and prosperity, as did also the country of Devadaha, over which Suprabuddha was reigning. This latter married a woman by the name of Lumbini, who was exceedingly fair; and in her company he was in the habit of visiting a beautiful grove near the city, which belonged to a wealthy citizen.

The Queen took such a fancy to the place, that she begged the King to give it to her. He told her he was not able to do so; but he had her one made more beautiful still, and it was called the Lumbini's grove. After a while Lumbini brought forth a child of such extraordinary and supernatural beauty that they called her Maya. Sometime later a second daughter was born, whom they called Mahamaya. Suprabuddha offered the hands of his daughters to Sihahanu for his son Suddhodana. He took

Mahamaya, for it had been predicted that she would bear a son with all the characteristics of a *chakravartin* monarch; but he was obliged, for the time being, to refuse the elder sister, on account of the *Cakya* law allowing a man only one wife. At that time the hillmen of the Pandava tribe (Shjahseng-hji-hii) were raiding the Sakya country, and the people begged the King to send his son Suddhodana to subdue them. The King consented, and the young prince vanquished them. Sihahanu requested that, as a recompense, they would allow his son to have two wives. The people allowed him this privilege, and Suddhodana married Maya.

After a while Sihahanu died, and Suddhodana reigned in his stead; and he knew Mahamaya as his wife; but she bore him no children. Now the future Buddha was in the Tushita heaven, and knowing that his time had come, he made the five preliminary examinations before being born on earth:

1. the proper family (in which to be born)
2. the country
3. the time
4. the race
5. the woman

Then, having decided that Mahamaya was the right mother, in the midnight watch he entered her womb under the appearance of an elephant.

Then the Queen had four dreams.

1. She saw a six-tusked white elephant enter her womb
2. She moved in space above

3. She ascended a great rocky mountain
4. A great multitude bowed down to her

The soothsayers predicted that she would bring forth a son with the thirty-two signs of a great man. If he stays at home, he will become a universal monarch, but if he shaves his hair and beard, and, putting on an orange-coloured robe, leaves his home for a homeless state and renounces the world, he will become a *Tathagata*, a perfectly enlightened Buddha.

While visiting the Lumbini garden, the pains of childbirth came upon her, and she seized hold of a wide-spreading Ashoka tree. The baby emerged from her right side, without causing her any pain. At that very moment, the heavens rejoiced. Then *Cataketu* (Indra) caused a violent rain to fall and a wind to blow, which dispersed all the crowd (of her attendants). Assuming the appearance of an old woman, he went to receive the new-born child in his lap.

The Bodhisattva, however, ordered him back, and then took seven steps in the direction of each of the cardinal points.

Looking to the east he said, 'I will reach the highest nirvana'.

To the south, 'I will be the first of all creatures'.

To the west, 'This will be my last birth'.

To the north, 'I will cross the ocean of existence' (1-8).

Such legends which are linked to the life of almost all prophets of the world are admitted to be of great historical values.

At the birth of Prince Siddhartha Gautama, brahmins had predicted that he would either become a world teacher or a world ruler. To prevent his son from turning to religious life, Suddhodana did not allow him to see death or suffering, and distracted him with luxury. So, during his childhood, he grew up and experienced a comfortable youth. When he was 29 years old, he saw for the first time in his life what became known in Buddhism as the four sights: an old man, a sick person, a corpse, an ascetic.

RENUNCIATION

Moved by all these experiences, the prince left the palace in the middle of the night to live the life of a wandering ascetic, leaving behind his just-born son Rahul and wife Yasodhara. He travelled to the river Anomiya with his charioteer Chandaka and horse Kanthaka, and cut off his hair. Leaving his servant and horse behind, he journeyed into the woods and changed into monk's robes and wandered for alms.

Buddha then went to Rajgriha the mountain fortress of the Magadhans. King Bimbisara, standing in his palace, saw him, and on seeing him, said: 'Look at this one, sirs. How handsome, stately, pure. How consummate his demeanour – mindful, his eyes downcast, looking only a plow-length before him, as one who's not from a lowly lineage. Send the royal messengers at once to see where this monk will go'.

He went from house to house – well-restrained, mindful, alert – his bowl filled quickly. Then completing his alms round, he left the city, headed for Mount Pandava. When the messengers reported that he was a prince, Bimbisara hurriedly, in a state chariot went forth towards the Pandava and reached there. With exchange of greetings the King spoke thus, 'Young art thou and delicate, a lad in his first youth. Fine is thy colour, like a high-born noble's'.

Buddha refused the wealth and the shelter that had been offered by King Bimbisara and took refuge in the mountain near Rajagriha.

–*Pabbaja Sutta*: The Going Forth, by Thanissaro Bhikkhu.

At this time in India there were many religious teachers. One of the best and most well-known was Alara Kalama. Buddha went to study under him. He stayed there and learnt many things, including meditation. He worked hard and eventually equalled his teacher in learning. Finally, Alara Kalama could not teach him any more and he said, 'You are the same as I am now. There is no difference between us. Stay here and take my place and teach my students with me'.

But the Buddha's quest was not satisfied and he left Alara Kalama and went in search of a new teacher.

At last, he found another great teacher, Uddaka, who was famous for his cleverness. Again, Buddha stayed there and learnt what Uddaka had to teach. The fundamental question he was searching for was the origin of suffering and how to stop it, prevent old age and death. Uddaka could not teach him those. Once more disappointed, he left him, making up his mind to struggle by himself until he found the cause of all the suffering of life.

The *Ariyapariyesana Sutta* (*Majjhima Nikaya* 26) describes how the Buddha, dissatisfied with the teachings of Alara Kalama and Uddaka Ramaputta, wandered further through Magadhan country, and then found an agreeable piece of ground which served for striving. He sat and meditated at a place called Bodh Gaya. The *sutta* says that only then did he attain *Nibbana* (1-9).

As was the common practice in those times, he observed austere self-mortification to find the truth. For this he consumed just a tiny portion of food each day and immersed in meditation.

But that self-mortification left him nowhere. One day while in meditation he suddenly fell unconscious and was about to die from his vigilant fasting.

Then he accepted a bowl of rice from a young girl named Sujata. Once he had eaten, he had a realisation that physical austerities were not the means to achieve spiritual liberation. Self-mortification would not help to reveal the truth he was seeking and so he returned to normal living.

This was considered a failure by the five ascetics who had followed him during his course of meditation. They believed that giving up self-mortification meant stepping away from the truth of salvation. They left him and went to Banaras.

THE AWAKENING

After defeating the forces of the demon Mara, Siddhartha reached enlightenment and became a Buddha at the age of 35.

Afterwards, he remained silent for forty-nine days. Then he came out with a firm resolve to preach his realisation to the world. For this, he initially intended to visit his former teachers, Alara Kalama and Uddaka Ramaputta, to teach them his insights, but they had already died. So he decided to visit his five former companions. On his way, he encountered a spiritual seeker named Upaka. The Buddha himself proclaimed that he had achieved full awakening, but Upaka was not convinced.

The Buddha then journeyed from Bodh Gaya to Sarnath, a small town near the sacred city of Varanasi in central India. There he met his five former companions, the ascetics with whom he had shared six years of hardship. They were suspicious at first of the Buddha. They did not greet him when he approached them.

They told him that since he had broken his vow and abandoned holiness, he was no more a *Bhikkhu* but Gautama, an ordinary man who lives in abundance and indulges in the pleasures of worldliness. Despite this disrespect, Gautam the Buddha now, approached them in a dignified manner and the five *bhikkhus* rose from their seats and received him. They were convinced and requested him to teach what he had learned. Thereupon the Buddha gave the teaching that was later recorded to be the *Dhammacakkappavattana Sutta*, which introduces the fundamental concepts of Buddhist thought, such as the Middle Way and the Four Noble Truths.

The five disciples were Kaundinya, Assaji, Bhaddiya, Vappa and Mahanama, all of them Brahmins who had known Siddharth in the past. They are known as the *Pancavaggiya bhikkhus.*

Then Buddha spoke to them, 'Do not call me by my name nor address me as a friend for I am the Buddha, the holy one'. Thereafter, he elaborated what he had achieved in meditation. He went on saying that he didn't seek salvation in austerities but he would also never indulge in worldly pleasures nor live in abundance. He the *Tathagata* has found the middle path.

He, then, preached his first sermon which is Dhamma *Cakkappavattana Sutta*. It is not easy to mention the exact date when this *sutta*, the first sermon was introduced.

Three months after the passing away of Buddha the first council was held in the deer sanctuary of Banaras. Venerable Mahakassapa (one of the foremost disciples of the Buddha known for his deep asceticism, wisdom, and leadership within the Buddhist monastic community) asked Venerable Ananda (another principal disciple of the Buddha) where the first *Dhammacakkappavattana* was first delivered. Ananda then told that at one time the blessed one was staying at Isipatana now known as Sarnath and the Enlightened One alighted from the sky, in the deer sanctuary, in the township of Banaras. Then the blessed one addressed the five *bhikkhus*.

THE WANDERING ASCETIC

For forty-five long years, till he attained *Mahaparinirvana* Gautam Buddha led the life of a wanderer, walking fifteen-twenty miles daily from village to village through the lower plains along the River Ganges, remaining in one place (usually near his home) for only three months during the rainy season.

After the first proclamation he came to Varanasi. It was on the full moon day of July, when he spent his first retreat at Varanasi (Isipatana). From there, he went to Rajgir (Rajagriha) and stayed in the *Benu vana* (Bamboo Grove) for three consecutive years. In the third year of his stay there, Sudatta, a householder of Savasthi known as *Anathapindika* (the feeder of the forlorn), came to meet him. He listened to him and developed immense faith in him. He remained devoted to the Buddha's teachings until he attained *Sotapatti* (the first stage of sainthood). He came to be known as the *Dayaka* (chief supporter) of the Master. Anathapindika built the famous Jetavana monastery at Savasthi, known as Sahet-mahet now, and offered it to the Buddha and his disciples. One can visit the ruins of this monastery even now.

Buddha then went to Vaishali in the fifth year. He heard about his father's illness and went to visit him. There he preached the Dhamma, hearing which enabled the king to attain *Arahat* (perfect sanctity) and after enjoying the bliss of emancipation for seven days, he passed away. The Order of Nuns was also founded during this time. In the sixth year he took retreat in Mankula Hill and performed *yamaka pathariya* (Twin Wonder). He did the same for the first time to overcome the pride of the Sakya-relatives. In the seventh year, the Buddha preached the *Abhidharma* or the Higher Doctrine in the *Tavatimsa* (the Heaven of the Thirty-three) in memory of his mother Mahamaya, who had passed away seven days after his birth and was supposed to be reborn as a deva in the *Tavatimsa*. In the eighth year, Nakulapita and his wife, a genial couple,met him in the Bhesakala Forest (near Sumsumarigiri). The prayer that they might continue to live together forever was blessed.

During the ninth year Buddha spent his life in Kosambi at the Ghosita Monastery and in the subsequent year in the Parileyakka Forest. During his stay there a dispute arose between two parties of monks owing to an offence committed by a monk. Buddha failed to resolve the dispute between the two adamant parties. However, they later came to Savasthi and begged for the pardon of the Buddha. The next year, Buddha met the brahmin farmer Kasi Bharadwaj who spoke to him somewhat discourteously but the Buddha answered his questions with patience and modesty. That made Bharadwaj an ardent follower of the Buddha. It was on this occasion that the very interesting discourse *Kasi Bharadwaj Sutta* (*Sutta Nipata*) was delivered.

During the twelfth year the *Vinaya* was introduced. It was also during this retreat that the brahmin Viraja came to see the Buddha, asked a series of questions on Buddhist practices, and was satisfied with the answers. He became a follower of the Buddha and invited the Master and the *Sangha* to spend the rainy season with him.

In the thirteenth year Elder Meghiya a disciple of the Buddha was attracted by a beautiful mango grove near a river and asked the Buddha for permission to go there for meditation. The over-enthusiastic Meghiya disobeyed Buddha's request to wait and went there to meditate but soon realised that that would harm him. Buddha, then, delivered advise such as five things that are conducive to their maturing: (1) a good friend; (2) virtuous behaviour guided by the essential precepts for training; (3) good counsel tending to dispassion, calm, cessation, enlightenment and nirvana; (4) the effort to abandon evil thoughts; (5) acquiring of wisdom that discerns the rise and fall of things.

He spent the fourteenth year, at Jetavana monastery, Savasthi and during this time the Venerable Rahul, who was still a *Samanera* (novice), received *Upasampada* (higher ordination).

Thus, he went on campaigning in the subsequent years. He spent the 21st- 43rd years at Savasthi. In the 44th year he became gravely ill and in the 45th year of his Enlightenment, the Buddha passed away at Kushinagar in the month of *Baisakh* (May) before the commencement of the rains.

The Buddha's life may be sketched thus:

- Birth;
- Four Significant Visions (old age, sickness, death, an ascetic);
- The Great Renunciation (leaving the palace to seek the truth);
- Self-Mortification (years of extreme ascetic practices);
- Final Triumph (attaining enlightenment);
- Dependent Arising (understanding the cause of suffering);
- First Sermon (teaching the Four Noble Truths);
- The Middle Path (balance between indulgence and self-denial);

- Spreading the Dharma (teaching others);
- Years of teaching (guiding disciples and communities);
- Buddhahood and Arahantship (liberation from suffering);
- *Parinirvana* (final passing away).

2

BUDDHA'S FIRST SERMON

The *Dhammacakkappavattana Sutta* (*The Discourse on the Turning of the Wheel of* Dhamma) is one of the most important Buddhist scriptures. The first exposition of the Four Noble Truths, it is traditionally considered to be the first sermon given by the Buddha after attaining enlightenment. The *sutta* was delivered to the five ascetics in the Deer Park at Sarnath.

Dhamma (Pali) or dharma (Sanskrit) here refers to the Buddha's teachings that leads to one's liberation from suffering. *Cakka* (Pali) or *cakra* (Sanskrit) can be interpreted as 'wheel'. The *dhammacakka* can be translated as Wheel of Dhamma that is a Buddhist symbol referring to Buddha's teaching of the path to enlightenment. *Pavattana* (Pali) or *Pabartana* can be translated as 'setting in motion'.

This wheel in motion signifies a great and revolutionary change, the ushering of a new era. Buddhaghosa, the 5th century Buddhist scholar and commentator explains that this wheel which the Buddha turned is primarily to be understood as wisdom, knowledge, and insight. This wisdom has two aspects, *pativedha-nana*, (wisdom of self-realisation of the Truth) and *desana-nana* (wisdom of proclamation of the Truth). *Pativedhanana* is further explained as that which is in the course of *uppajjamanam* (being realised) and *uppannam* (that which is realised).

From the time when the Bodhisatta as the hermit Sumedha sitting at the feet of the former Buddha Dipankar resolved to achieve perfection, up to the time of realisation of the Path of Arhantship, the *dhammacakka* is described as being in the course of realisation. The *dhammacakka* was realised when he finally realised the *arahatta phala* (fruit of Arhantship) at the Bodhi-mandala.

As the ideal wheel of the universal monarch, it assists him to conquer the world by righteous means. It is his *Ajna-cakra* (symbol of inner power). The dharmachakra symbol also points to the central Indian idea of 'Dharma', a complex and multivalent term which refers to the eternal cosmic law, and the universal moral order. In Buddhism it refers to the very teaching and the path expounded by the Buddha's teachings, *samsara* (cycle of birth and rebirth), and the *paticcasamuppada* (law of cause and effect). It also symbolises the Buddha as *Dhammakaya* (truth body) and the power of a just ruler. Over time, it became the main emblem of Buddhism, signifying both its philosophy and spiritual path (2-1).

Ancients described the wheel – both in the sense of ratana-cakka as well as dhamma-cakka as:

Cittīkataṃ mahagghanca – atulam dullabha (2-1- Page 34).

It means rich in ornamentation, incalculable in value,uparalleled, a sight rarely seen, associated solely with supreme beings. It is aptly called Ratana, a gem supreme.

The Middle Path

This passage is from the teachings of the Buddha and explains the *majjhima pratipada* (Middle Path). *Tathagata*, the Buddha, advised *Bhikkhus* who have gone forth from worldly life not to indulge in the two extreme paths.

Anariya (Chasing worldly pleasures like wealth, sensual enjoyment, and luxury) – This is inferior and unhelpful for spiritual growth. Self-indulgence is unworthy, vain and fit only for the worldly-minded. This extreme practice of taking delight in desirable objects, pursuing and enjoying sensuous pleasures is low, vulgar, and the habit of village and town folks, indulged in by the ordinary common worldlings. It is not pursued by the Noble One. It's ignoble, unclean, not tending to the true interests one is seeking after. Such pursuit after sensuous pleasure is an extreme practice *Bhikkhus* should avoid.

Dukkha (Self-mortification or extreme self-denial) – The other extreme practice of inflicting torture on oneself can result in suffering only. Abstaining from food and clothing which are normally needed for the living is self-torture and it can produce nothing. This self-mortification should also be avoided. Punishing the body through excessive fasting, pain, or suffering, thinking it will bring spiritual enlightenment is also not beneficial, according to the Buddha.

Instead of these two extremes, the Buddha discovered the *Majjhima* (Middle Path – a balanced way of life) that leads to wisdom, inner peace, and ultimately nirvana (liberation from suffering). This path helps in understanding life better, gaining *nana* (deep knowledge), and achieving *Sambodhi* (enlightenment).

According to the Buddha, the blessed one, neither abstinence from flesh, nor going naked, nor shaving the head, nor wearing matted hair, nor dressing in a rough garment, nor covering oneself with dirt, nor sacrificing to Agni, will cleanse a man who is not free from delusions. Reading the Vedas, making offerings to priest, or sacrifices to the gods, self-mortification by heat or cold, and many such penances performed for the sake of immortality do not cleanse the man who is not free from delusions. Anger, drunkenness, obstinacy, bigotry, deception, envy, self-praise, disparaging others, superciliousness and evil intentions constitute uncleanness.

The opening lines of the first sermon can be interpreted as a warning for those *bhikkhus* who have gone forth from worldly life. They should not indulge in these two extreme paths of self-indulgence and self-mortification. A *bhikkhu* should be immune from such defilement as lust and anger that only begets lust and anger for them. They should take control of their sense organs and regulate them. An ordinary person indulges in pleasurable sights and they practice and pursue sensuality. Again, all sources of sound, smell and touch or even material objects that men and women come in contact with also constitute sensuousness.

The *Noble Eightfold Path*

According to *Dhamma-cakka-Pavattana Sutta* 2, The Buddha said: It is, *bhikkhus*, the Noble Eightfold Path, that is to say:

1. *Samma-ditthi* (Right View) – understanding the nature of reality and the path of transformation.
2. *Samma-sankappa* (Right Resolve) – commitment to ethical and mental self improvement.

3. *Samma-vaca* (Right Speech) – speaking truthfully, kindly, and helpfully.
4. *Samma-kammanta* (Right Action) – behaving peacefully and harmoniously; refraining from harm.
5. *Samma-ajiva* (Right Livelihood) – earning a living in a way that does not harm others.
6. *Samma-vayama* (Right Effort) – cultivating positive states of mind; freeing oneself from unwholesome states.
7. *Samma-sati* (Right Mindfulness) – developing awareness of the body, feelings, mind, and phenomena.
8. *Samma-samadhi* (Right Concentration) – developing deep states of meditative absorption (*jhana*).

This, *bhikkhus*, is the *majjhima patipada* to which the *Tathagata* has awakened, which produces vision, which produces nana, and leads to appeasement, to *abhinna*, to *sambodhi*, to *nibbana*.

The Buddha realised the arya-satyas in the fourth *jhana* (dhyana), when he got engrossed in a state of deep meditative calm. He could, then, remember many of his past lives and realise how beings were reborn according to the ethical quality of their *karmas* (actions). Wandering for countless lives in the various realms of rebirth through *karma* would naturally lead to an enhanced awareness both of the forces leading to repeated rebirths and of their attendant *dukkha*. The rebirths are long-lasting but not eternal and have their various pains.

Buddhist literature contains elaborate interpretations of Buddhist scholars. What Buddha had taken to teach the common people was a slow but step by step discourse. He initiated talk on common virtues like *dana* (charity)and *sila* (virtue). He explained why people should avoid sensual pleasures and how it accelerates the inferior nature and thus advised them to renounce that inferior nature. When he came to realise that Upali the householder was free from sense pleasures, immune of ill will and vacillation, confident and fit for receiving the discourse, he revealed to him the Dharma.

The main essence of the teaching was *dukkha*, its origin and cause, the way to be adopted for its cessation.

Dukkha is often translated as suffering which however, represents only one aspect of *dukkha*, a term whose range of implications is difficult to capture with a single English word. *Dukkha* can be derived from the Sanskrit *kha*, one meaning of which is the axle-hole of a wheel and the antithetic prefix *dua* (dus), which stands for 'difficulty' or 'badness'. The complete term then evokes the image of an axle not fitting properly into its hole. According to this image, *dukkha* suggests 'disharmony' or 'friction'. Alternatively, *dukkha* can be related to the Sanskrit *stha,* 'standing' or 'abiding', combined with the same antithetic prefix dua. *Dukkha* in the sense of 'standing badly' then conveys nuances of uneasiness or of being uncomfortable. In order to catch the various nuances of *dukkha*, the most convenient translation is 'unsatisfactoriness', though it might be best to leave the term untranslated (2-3).

The term *sacca* or satya which is regularly used in the sense of truth, is qualified by ariya or arya, meaning what is real and what has 'a genuine real existence'. The Sanskrit word satya is related to the word 'sat' meaning 'existence or being', and both can have religious connotations. In the pre-Buddhist Upanishads, sat (being) is equated with atman (self) and Brahman who is taken to be the unchanging essence of a person and the world.

Another interpretation is given by Bhikkhu Bodhi which can be mentioned here. The word ariya or 'noble', is used by the Buddha to designate a particular type of person, the type of person which it is the aim of his teaching to create. In the discourses the Buddha classifies human beings into two broad categories. On one side there are the *puthujjana*, the worldlings, those belonging to the multitude, whose eyes are still covered with the dust of defilements and delusion. On the other side there are the *Aryans*, the noble ones, the spiritual elite, who obtain this status not from birth, social station or ecclesiastical authority but from their inward nobility of character. The noble ones do not flow along thoughtlessly with the stream of life, but endeavour to comprehend existence from within, as honestly and thoroughly as possible.

These two general types are not separated from each other by an impassable chasm, each confined to a tightly sealed compartment. A series of gradations can be discerned rising up from the darkest level of the blind worlding trapped in the dungeon of egotism and self-assertion, through the stage of the virtuous worlding in whom the seeds of wisdom are beginning to sprout, and further through the intermediate stages of noble disciples to the perfected individual at the apex of the entire scale of human development. This is the *arahant*, the liberated one, who has absorbed the purifying vision of truth so deeply that all his defilements have been extinguished, and with them, all liability to suffering (2-4).

Buddha had to undergo strenuous striving for six years in his last phase of meditation when at last he attained the Truth of 'Supreme Enlightenment' under the Bodhi tree in Bodhgaya. What he realised as Truths after his enlightenment, constitute the essence of the dhamma (Teaching). So, in Buddhism, Buddha is 'the Noble One' to be called 'The Buddha'.

In the Brahminic system, the term ariya refers to members of the top three of the four social classes as pure of descent and social superiority.

Others who are 'Noble' fall into four categories:

a. Who have had direct experiential insight into all four ariya *saccas*. They cannot be reborn at less than a human level, and will become fully enlightened within seven lives at most.
b. Whose insight has weakened the fetters of desire for sense – pleasures and ill-will. Their future rebirths can only include one in the sense – desire realms of humans and the lower heavens.
c. Who have ended the latter two fetters. They can only be reborn in the higher heavens, where they in time become fully enlightened.
d. Who are fully enlightened beings called *arahats* having ended the final fetters of attachment to any heavenly realms or experiences. They are free from restlessness, conceit and ignorance and thus experience nirvana and cannot be reborn in any form.

CHATURARYASATYA (THE FOUR NOBLE TRUTHS)

These four truths form the foundation of Buddhist teachings:

- *Dukkha* – Truth of Suffering;
- *Samudaya* – Truth of the Origin of Suffering (Craving/ Tanha);
- *Nirodha* – Truth of the Cessation of Suffering;

- *Marga* – Truth of the Path to the Cessation of Suffering which is the Noble Eightfold Path;

1. *Dukkha* (Truth of Suffering)

Dukkha – The core structure of early Buddhist teachings follows this pattern of various forms of *dukkha* or suffering, physical or mental, and should be fully understood. For us, too, it is necessary to reflect upon the nature of our life. We must attempt to fathom the deep significance of an existence bound on one side by birth and on the other by death, and subject in between to all the types of suffering.

The eleven types of suffering are:

a. *Jati* (Birth) is suffering because by the birth of a being is meant the genesis of the new mind. With the new existence, there is the appearance of physical and mental suffering throughout the whole of the ensuing existence. Birth, therefore, is considered as suffering.
b. *Jara* (Aging) means the body is gradually weakening and decaying. The hair turns gray, skin wrinkles, the body bends, hearing and eyesight decline. Mentally, memory fades, reactions slow, and the senses weaken, leading to physical and mental suffering.
c. *Marana* (Death) is suffering as it implies the end of the continuous cycle of life that has been ongoing since birth. Before death there comes naturally an acute pain that one is to leave his dear and near ones forever. Again, as death approaches, one is subject to severe attacks of disease and illness and unbearable pain. It, therefore, has been, included in '*dukkha*'.

d. *Soka* (Sorrow) is the suffering caused by life events such as losing loved ones, losing property, declining health, moral failures, or adopting wrong views. It is a form of mental distress with suffering as its core nature. Therefore, sorrow is fearsome and is named *dukkha* by the Buddha.

e. *Pariveda* (Lamentation) is suffering caused by loss, whether of loved ones, property, or other misfortunes. It leads to wailing and distress, causing physical pain. The Buddha declared lamentation as suffering, as crying brings pain and sorrow.

f. *Dukkha* (Physical pain) such as stiffness, aches, soreness, fatigue, itchiness, and feeling hot or cold, is a form of suffering. This true intrinsic suffering is called *dukkha-dukkha*. Even animals fear physical pain. Sickness and disease also fall under this category. Physical pain often leads to mental distress, making it a cause of further suffering, which is why it is called *dukkha*, meaning dreadful suffering.

g. *Domanassa* (Mental displeasure) is a form of suffering. The Pali word domanassa means mental pain or distress. It includes worry, anxiety, depression, dislike, hatred, fear, and misery. As a form of intrinsic suffering, it arises from negative mental states and emotional distress.

h. *Upayasa* (Despair or dejection) is suffering as it is affected by the loss of loved ones, property and any other losses or suffering and brings excessive mental agony. It is, therefore, intense *dukkha* that may end in insanity or suicide.

i. *Sakhara-dukkha* (Association with the hateful) refers to the suffering caused by conditioned existence, including emotional and mental struggles such as being forced into unpleasant situations or relationships. This specific suffering is also mentioned in the phrase *appiyehi sampayogo dukkho* (association with the hateful is suffering) from Buddhist texts.

j. *Piyehi vippayogo* (Separation from the beloved) is suffering. It may happen through death, serious illness, or the loss of cherished possessions, causing deep mental agony. As it leads to various emotional afflictions, the Buddha called it *dukkha*, or dreadful suffering.

k. *Yampiccham̦ na labhati tampi* (Not getting what one desires) is suffering because unfulfilled desires lead to pain, disappointment, and despair, sometimes even driving people to extreme actions like suicide.

The eleven types of suffering, starting from the suffering of birth to the suffering of not getting what one wants, are all obvious types of suffering known as *dukkha-dukkha* (intrinsic suffering). They arise because of feelings, perceptions, volitional activities and consciousness aggregates. Without them, such suffering will not arise.

Happiness is temporary. Thus, even pleasure leads to suffering when it is destroyed. Pleasant experiences, whether physical or mental, do not last forever. Pleasurable physical sensations and joyful states of mind please all beings but when this blissful contentment disappears or gets destroyed, it causes agony. This is the *Viparinama-Dukkha* (suffering due to change). For example, when one suddenly loses their accumulated wealth or when someone dear dies, or when one is separated from a loved one, it brings immense distress and deep penetrating grief. Thus, these two forms of happiness namely pleasant physical and mental feelings are also a type of suffering because of change (2-4).

Thus, everything in life is dependent on causes and conditions. Since nothing is permanent, relying on anything for happiness is futile.

2. *Samudaya* (Noble Truth of the Origin of Suffering)

Tanha **(Craving)** – According to the Buddha, the Noble Truth of the Origin of Suffering is *Tanha* or Craving. It means an irresistible desire mainly moved by pleasure and greed and it goes unending from birth to birth.

Tanha or Craving are three of three kinds:

a. *Kama-tanha*, the sensual craving for bodily pleasure,
b. *Bhava-Tanha*, the craving for eternal existence,
c. *Vibhava-Tanha*, the craving for non-existence or self-annihilation.

a. *Kama-Tanha* (Sensual Craving): The six sense objects – visible objects, sounds, smells, tastes, touch, and mental objects – form the basis of human experience. These objects give rise to six types of consciousness: seeing, hearing, smelling, tasting, touching, and thinking. When the senses come into contact with their respective objects, they generate corresponding sensory impressions. Sensual craving can take different forms such as enjoying beauty, pleasant sounds, fragrances, delicious food, pleasurable touch, or even wishing for a higher existence to indulge in more pleasures. However, this craving is rooted in ignorance, where impermanence is mistaken for permanence, suffering for happiness, and the non-self for self.

According to Buddhist teachings, this cycle of sensory experience and craving explains the Noble Truth of the Origin of Suffering, as attachment to fleeting sensory pleasures binds individuals to the cycle of birth, suffering, and rebirth.

b. *Bhava-Tanha* (craving for eternal existence), is the belief that life or the soul is permanent and continues even after the body dies. It assumes that even if the physical world disappears, the soul remains eternal. Before the Buddha's teachings, many believed that after death, a person either remained in heaven or suffered in hell forever, based on divine will. Others thought that beings moved from one life to another according to *karma*, existing indefinitely.

This craving makes people desire a good and prosperous life, both in the present and future, believing they will be reborn into better conditions. However, this attachment to life leads to suffering, as it fuels the cycle of rebirth and the five Aggregates of Clinging, which are impermanent. Thus, the Buddha identified Bhava-Tanha as a cause of suffering in the Noble Truth of the Origin of Suffering.

c. *Vibhava-Tanha* (craving for non-existence), is the belief that nothing exists after death and that life only matters while one is alive. This belief leads people away from doing good deeds, as they think life ends completely at death, so they should enjoy it without concern for consequences.

Such thinking encourages reckless behaviour, ignoring morality and responsibility. It can lead to a nihilistic outlook, where people do whatever they want without caring about right or wrong. In this way, the craving for non-existence becomes a cause of suffering, as explained in the Noble Truth of the Origin of Suffering.

The significance of the Second Noble Truth is the concept of *anicca* (impermanence) that states that nothing in the universe, not even the Self is permanent or unchanging. Not suffering, but even positive desires perpetuate the cycle of reincarnation and *dukkha*.

3. *Nirodha* (Noble Truth of the Cessation of Suffering)

The third 'True Reality' described in the DCPS is as follows:

'Now this, monks, for the spiritually ennobled, is the ceasing-of-the-painful true reality. It is the remainder less fading away and cessation of that same craving, the giving up and relinquishing of it, freedom from it, non-reliance on it.'

The **Truth of the Cessation of Suffering** is to extinct the origin of craving. There are four stages in the extinction of craving.

1. *Sotapanna* or stream-winner. It is the First Stage of Sainthood. One entering the stream comes to realise that he has entered the stream that leads to nirvana. For the *Sotapanna*, all the worldly cravings are closed forever and he will never retreat to a worlding again. He is now on the way to attain Arhantship and enter nirvana.

There are three types of *Sotapanna*:

a. *Ekabiji-Sotapanna* – one who enters nirvana after one life.
b. *Kolamkola-Sotapanna* – one who enters nirvana after two to six lives.
c. *Sattakkhattu-parama-Sotapanna* – one who enters nirvana after seven lives.

2. *Sakadagami*: It is the second stage of sainthood that means 'once returner'. During this second stage of sainthood the *Sakadagami* has weakened the grip of Tanha and *Vyapada* (ill will), though these defilements have not been entirely eradicated. That is, in *Sakadagami* one acquires the knowledge that leads him to the extent that he will suffer not more than one rebirth in the sensual plane before attaining Arhantship or full enlightenment. Compared to the *Sotapanna*, he is nobler in *Sakadagami* and is much closer to liberation. While a *Sotapanna* has eradicated doubt, belief in a permanent self, and attachment to rituals, a *Sakadagami* has further weakened the desires and aversions that bind one to suffering. This stage represents significant spiritual progress, moving closer to the final goal of nirvana.
3. *Anagamin*: It is the third stage of sainthood. In *Anagamin*, one destroys the fetters of ill-will and sensual cravings and he will be devoid of anger or hatred or any other worldlings.
4. *Arahant*: The final stage of sainthood. An *Arahant* (Arhat) has completely destroyed all forms of craving and eradicated all the *Samyojanas* (Fetters) that bind one to existence. An *arahant*'s mind is in the purest state, immune from any defilements. Now he is the noblest saint who has no craving for enjoying the present life as well as future lives.

The DCPS also describes this path as a 'middle way' (*majjhima paipada* or *madhyama pratipad*) which avoids two extremes – the pursuit of sensual pleasures and self-mortification. The path involves wisdom, moral virtue, and meditative training (2-5).

Therefore, we must understand the Third Noble Truth which says the only way to be freed from the cycle of suffering, death, and rebirth is by completely eliminating desires for temporal things. Gautam Buddha left home to find what is wrong with mankind and how can it be corrected. The answer lies in eliminating absolutely all desires, good or bad.

4. *Marga* – (The Truth of the Path to the Cessation of Suffering) – The Noble Eightfold Path

Once we have grasped the fact that all conditioned things in the world, being impermanent and insubstantial, can never give us total satisfaction, we can then lift our aim to the unconditioned element, nirvana the Deathless, as our focal point.

To achieve the fourth noble truth, the Noble Eightfold Path is assigned for us. Birth is exhausted, the Holy Life has been lived out, what was to be done is done, there is no more of this to come. Now, comes nirvana, the Noble Truth of the Cessation of Suffering. This is said thus: now this, monks, for the spiritually ennobled, is the true reality which is the way leading to the cessation of the painful. It is this noble eight-factored path, that is to say, (1) right view, (2) right resolve, (3) right speech, (4) right action, (5) right livelihood, (6) right effort, (7) right mindfulness, (8) right mental unification.

This is too difficult for the common man to reach; the Buddha's teaching gives us the meticulous instructions that we need to tread the path culminating in the plane of the noble ones. 'This is the path that gives birth to vision, that gives birth to knowledge, that leads to higher comprehension, enlightenment and *Nibbana*, the crowning attainment of nobility (2-6).'

The *Dhammacakkappavattana Sutta* describes three stages of understanding for each of the four realities, leading to twelve insights:

1. *Sacca-nana* – knowing the truth.
2. *Kicca- nana* – understanding what needs to be done.
3. *Kata- nana* – accomplishing what needs to be done.

These three stages form the foundation of the Theravada tradition and are also acknowledged by some contemporary Mahayana teachers.

*PANCUPADANAKHANDA (*FIVE AGGREGATES OR GROUPS)

The *Upadana-khandhas* (Five Bundles of Grasping-Fuel) are the five aggregates (*khandhas*) that a person clings to, fueling suffering and rebirth. According to DCPS, these five factors make up a person, each being both a khandha or bundle as well an upadana or an object of grasping. However, upadana itself is a mental state, not five separate types of grasping. A sentient being is made up of the *Pancupanakhanda (*Five Aggregates or Groups) that form the objects of clinging or grasping. In Buddhism these five components make up the human experience and are the basis for attachment and suffering.

Here the word Upadana may be taken as 'fuel' which keeps up the fire. Richard Gombrich a renowned British scholar of Buddhism and Indology comments that the *suttas* are rich in fire-related metaphors due to the importance of fire in Brahmanism, and then argues that the term upadana-khandha is also part of this fire imagery (2-7). The upadana-khandhas, then, can each be seen as a 'bundle of fuel' which 'burn' with the 'fires' of *dukkha* and its causes. Therefore, to a spiritually ennobled person, the understanding of reality is different from that of ordinary people. Nirvana as the blissful state beyond all conditioned phenomena of the round of rebirths.

Again, from the material aspects, the five *Upadana-khandhas* are assumed as – matter, sensations, perception, formations, and consciousness. These five bundles or aggregates make up the physical and mental existence of each person. In Buddhist and ancient Indian philosophy, the *Mahabhuta* (four basic elements) are the fundamental components of physical existence. They are:

1. *Pathavi* (Earth) – Represents solidity, stability, and structure (e. g. , bones, flesh).
2. *Apo* (Water) – Represents fluidity, cohesion, and binding (e. g. , blood, saliva).
3. *Tejo* (Fire) – Represents heat, energy, and transformation (e. g. , metabolism, digestion).
4. *Vayo* (Air) – Represents movement, motion, and breath (e. g. , respiration, circulation).

These elements are not separate substances but qualities present in all physical phenomena, including the human body. Some Buddhist traditions also add a fifth element, *Akasa* (Space), as the container for all existence.

The five *Upadana-khandhas* are:

1. *Rupa* (Form/Material Aggregate) – The physical body and external matter, including the five senses. When the

eye comes into contact with an external object, visual perception begins.

2. *Vedana* (Feeling/Sensation Aggregate) – The sensations (pleasant, unpleasant, or neutral) that arise from contact with objects. *Sukha-vedana* (pleasant feeling), *dukkha-vedana* (unpleasant feeling), or *upekkha-vedana* (neutral feeling) arises based on the object seen.
3. *Sanna* (Perception Aggregate) – The ability to recognize and identify objects, concepts, and experiences. It classifies and labels the object based on past experiences.
4. *Sankara* (Mental Formations/VolitionalActivitiesAggregate) – The mental reactions, habits, and karmic tendencies that shape one's character. *Manusikara* (attention) turns toward the object. *Cetana* (volition) initiates reactions such as attraction, aversion, or neutrality. These mental formations lead to *karma* (wholesome or unwholesome actions).
5. *Vinnana* (Consciousness Aggregate) – Awareness or cognition that arises from sense perception. *Cakkhuvinnaṇa* (eye-consciousness) arises, simply registering that an object is seen. It is the awareness of visual perception without interpretation.

These five aggregates which wc mistakenly identify as self lead to attachment. This clinging leads to suffering and is a core teaching in Buddhist philosophy. Understanding and seeing through them is the key to achieving *Nibbana* (liberation).

In a nutshell, the basic concept in Buddhism is that everything is changeable and nothing is permanent but it is nirvana that is unchanging and permanent. As things are impermanent, they are also *dukkha* or painful. Again, *dukkha*s are to be seen as *anatta* (non-self). When something is said to be *anatta*, it is painful and impermanent. It is often interpreted as a doctrine denying the existence of a self, but it is more accurately described as a strategy to attain non-attachment by recognizing everything as impermanent.

Anatta (Pali) is synonymous with *Anatmam* in Sanskrit Buddhist texts. Unlike Vedic beliefs in a permanent Atman (true self), Buddhism teaches that nothing has a lasting essence. *Anatta* also means that nothing truly belongs to a self – it is *Sunna* or empty (2-8).

The concept of *Anatta* appears in numerous *Sutras* of the ancient Buddhist Nikaya texts (Pali canon). It appears, for example, as a noun in *Samyutta Nikaya, Anguttara Nikaya, Patisambhidamagga, and Dhammapada*. It also appears as an adjective, for example, in *Samyutta Nikaya*, in *Sutta* and *Vinaya*.

According to Steven Collins, the inquiry of *anatta* and 'denial of self' in the canonical Buddhist texts is 'insisted on only in certain theoretical contexts', while they use the terms *atta, purisa, puggala* quite naturally and freely in various contexts. The elaboration of the *anatta* doctrine, along with identification of the words such as '*puggala*' as 'permanent subject or soul' appears in later Buddhist literature (2-9).

This important teaching was the *Anatta-lakkhana Sutta* introduced in the second sermon. Here he explained, with respect to each of the five khandhas, that, if it were truly Self, it would not 'tend to sickness,' and it would be totally controllable at will. Khandha, being *dukkha*, is changeable and so thinking as 'This is mine, this am I, this is my Self' is inappropriate and this thought will lead to *dukkha*.

The Buddha used the word self in everyday speech. This teaching does not deny continuity in life or across lives – character traits persist due to repeated *cittas* (mental patterns).

A person is simply a changing mix of mental and physical processes, with limited control over them.

As Peter Harvey observes, the non-Self teaching can easily be misunderstood so it is important to clarify it. The Buddha accepted many conventional usages of the word 'self' but rejected the idea of a permanent, independent Self. The non-Self teaching does not deny that there is continuity of character in life, and to some extent from life to life. But persistent character traits are due merely to the repeated occurrence of certain cittas, or mind-sets. A person, therefore, is a collection of rapidly changing and interacting mental and physical processes, with character patterns reoccurring over time. Only partial control can be exercised over these processes (2-2).

The concept of 'non-Self' can in fact be a way to overcome the negativity that attachment creates and help one to destroy frustration and a sense of loss, enabling them to go in for attaining nirvana.

So, the key origin or cause of *dukkha* is clinging to desires. Now desires are anyhow, to be satisfied. So, one hankers after gratification. Craving brings frustration and then pain and pain leads to quarrels, strife, and conflict between individuals and groups and motivates people to perform various actions. This brings further rebirths, thereby *dukkha*.

Nirvana literally means 'extinction', or extinction of a fire. This is described in the 'Fire sermon'. When Buddha proceeded from Urubela on his wandering in the direction of Gaya and reaching there addressed thousands of priests, he said, 'All things o' priests, are on fire... It is the eye, the ear, the nose, the tongue, the mind, the idea, the impressions... on fire. And with what are these on fire? With the fire of passion, say I, with the fire of hatred, with the fire of infatuation, with birth, old age, death, sorrow, lamentation, misery, grief and despair, are they on fire'. Buddha says that he is able, without moving his body, to 'stay experiencing nothing but *Sukha* (happiness) for up to seven days and nights'.

Thus, this teaches that everything internal and external to a person is burning with the fires of attachment, hatred, delusion, and of birth, aging, and death. Here the fires refer both to the causes of *dukkha* and to *dukkha* itself. Nirvana during life is frequently defined as the destruction of the three 'fires' or defilements. When one who has destroyed these dies, they cannot be reborn and so is totally beyond the remaining fires of birth, aging, and death, having attained final nirvana.

When the Buddha was asked if an enlightened person, after death, 'is', 'is not', both, or neither of these, he set the questions aside as irrelevant to the spiritual quest. There has been much speculation on what the Buddha's silence on this matter might imply (2-2-Harvey 1995, 208–10, 239–45; 2013, 78–80).

The path of early Buddhism and the Theravada school aims initially at lessening the mental pain that the vicissitudes and stresses of life can produce but ultimately at ending the round of rebirths, conditioned existence, and both its physical pains and its more subtly painful nature. The Mahayana tradition, though, does not see things of the world as painful by their very nature, for when truly understood with wisdom they are seen as non-different from nirvana. Hence the idea developed in the Mahayana that a buddha, and those advanced on the bodhisattva path leading to Buddhahood, could remain in, or in contact with, the world in what is known as *apratihita* (non-abiding) nirvana, clinging neither to the world of rebirths nor to nirvana as something supposedly separate from this.

3

BUDDHIST CANONICAL TEXTS

Buddha offered his teachings orally. No written scripts by Buddha have been found since it was not a tradition then. Several months after his demise, five hundred awakened disciples assembled at Rajagriha in an assembly. They recalled and recited the teachings from their memory. A large portion of Early Buddhist literature is part of the *sutra* genre delivered by the Buddha or by his close disciples. They are considered to be Buddha *vacana* by all schools. The Buddha's discourses or Buddha vacanas were later organized into collections called *Nikayas* (volumes) or *Agamas* meaning scriptures (3-2). They were further collected into the *Sutra Pitaka* (Basket of Discourses) of the canons of the early Buddhist schools.

With the gradual spread of Buddhism in the Indian subcontinent, the oral teachings came to get different dimensions. Consequently, different schools of Buddhism were established. Those were written down and thus we come to get the collections of scriptural texts.

Buddhist literature has made significant contributions to Indian culture and literature. The earliest Buddhist manuscripts consisting of a set of twenty-nine scrolls was recently found and it was preserved by the British Library. The script is the fragmentary birch bark scrolls, which were found inside one of a set of inscribed clay pots. They were written in the Gandhari Prakrit language (3-1) and in the Kharosthi script. It was dated to be from around the beginning of the Christian era.

Important Buddhist scripts were found in Gandhara (present-day northern Pakistan and eastern Afghanistan), once the capital of a series of wealthy and powerful dynasties. It was one of the world's most important centres of Buddhism. It was also the gateway through which Buddhism was transmitted from India to China and other parts of Asia. Gandhara was also a principal point of contact between India and the Western world (3-1). This volume introduces the Gandharan texts with interpretation and a detailed description of the manuscripts. It also carries a survey of their contents. It will open an enlightened discussion on Buddhism and how it was transmitted from India to other parts of central and eastern Asia. We cannot find all of Buddhism in one single textual collection.

THERAVADA SCHOOL OF BUDDHISM

The Theravada school of Buddhism, meaning 'Teaching of the Elders' is the oldest surviving branch of the Buddhist tradition. It originated around the third century BCE, following the Third Buddhist Council convened under Emperor Ashoka. Theravada traces its teachings to the Pali Canon which its followers regard as the most authentic record of the Buddha's discourses. This school emphasizes individual effort as the path to nirvana advocating a disciplined life rooted in ethical conduct, meditation, and the cultivation of wisdom. Its ultimate goal is to become an *arahant* – a person who has achieved enlightenment and is free from the cycle of rebirth. The school was established in Sri Lanka in the latter half of the first century BCE but also remained active in Andhra and other parts of South India, such as *Vana Vasa* in modern Karnataka, and later across South-East Asia. The school survived in Sri Lanka and established three main branches: The *Maha Vihara,* a prominent monastic centre established in Anuradhapura, Sri Lanka. It is generally regarded as the original stronghold of orthodox Theravada Buddhism and played a crucial role in preserving the Pali Canon and monastic discipline. From the *Maha Vihara* emerged other influential monastic traditions, notably the *Abhayagiri Vihara,* which arose in the first century BCE. Although it originated from the *Maha Vihara*, the *Abhayagiri* tradition later incorporated a broader range of teachings, including elements from Mahayana Buddhism. Another significant monastery was the *Jetavana Vihara,* which also emerged as a separate centre of Buddhist learning and practice in Sri Lanka. Over time, doctrinal and disciplinary differences led to distinctions between these monastic orders. However, it was the *Maha Vihara* tradition that ultimately came to represent the orthodox Theravada lineage, particularly after reforms and royal patronage in later centuries consolidated its authority and suppressed rival schools.

Theravada Buddhism is predominantly practised in Sri Lanka, Thailand, Myanmar, Laos, and Cambodia, where it continues to play a central role in spiritual and cultural life. Theravada remains more conservative and monastic in orientation, focusing on personal salvation through disciplined practice.

The later Mahayana tradition highlights the role of bodhisattvas and places greater emphasis on lay participation.

Chinese Buddhism focuses on studying Mahayana *sutras* and Mahayana treatises and draws its main doctrines from these sources. Some of the most important scriptures in Chinese Buddhism include: Lotus *Sutra*, Flower Ornament *Sutra*, Vimala Kirti *Sutra*, *nirvana Sutra*, and Amitabha *Sutra*. Chinese Buddhism is the largest institutionalized religion in mainland China.

Tibetan Buddhism has had a profound influence on global spirituality, with Tibetan masters bringing their teachings to the West. Tibetan Buddhism is a unique form of Mahayana Buddhism that incorporates *Vajrayana* (Tantric Buddhism) and elements of Tibetan culture. Practised mainly in Tibet, Bhutan, Mongolia, Nepal, Ladakh, and parts of Russia and China, it evolved from Indian Buddhism, particularly the teachings of Nalanda Monastery. Tibetan Buddhism preserves many scriptures that were lost in India after Buddhism declined there. It combines Mahayana's emphasis on compassion and enlightenment for all beings with Vajrayana's esoteric rituals and meditative techniques. It makes extensive use of *mantras*, *mandalas*, *mudras*, and *thangkas* (sacred paintings) in spiritual practice. A significant feature of Tibetan Buddhism is the Guru (Lama) lineage, where disciples receive guidance from enlightened masters, and the tulku system, which recognizes reincarnated teachers such as the Dalai Lama and Panchen Lama.

The tradition is divided into four major schools–

i. *Nyingma*, the oldest, emphasizing *Dzogchen* (Great Perfection);
ii. *Kagyu*, known for oral transmission and meditative practices like Mahamudra;
iii. *Sakya*, famous for its *Lamdre* (Path and Result) teachings;
iv. *Gelug*, the school of the Dalai Lama, which stresses monastic discipline, logic, and gradual path teachings.

The Three Canons of Buddhism refer to the major collections of scriptures preserved by different Buddhist traditions. Each canon reflects the doctrinal developments and cultural adaptations of Buddhism in different regions. These Canons are:

1. Pali Canon

The Pali Canon of the Theravada tradition, known as the *Tripitaka* in Sanskrit, is the primary Buddhist scripture. It consists of three Pitakas: *Vinaya Pitaka*, *Sutta Pitaka*, and *Abhidhamma Pitaka*.

Vinaya Pitaka outlines monastic discipline and is divided into three sections-*Khandhaka, Suttavibhanga,* and *Parivara.*

Sutta Pitaka comprises over ten thousand *sutras* related to Buddha and his close disciples, categorized into *Digha Nikaya, Anguttara Nikaya, Majjhima Nikaya, Khuddaka Nikaya,* and *Samyutta Nikaya.*

Abhidhamma Pitaka contains Buddhist doctrine and philosophy, divided into seven books: *Dhatukatha, Dhammasangani, Patthana, Kathavatthu, Vibhanga, Puggalapannatti,* and *Yamaka.*

2. Chinese Buddhist Canon

The Chinese Buddhist Canon is an organized collection of early Buddhist texts with Mahayana *sutras*, commentaries, and other texts from Indian and central Asian regions translated into or written in Chinese. Its content is supplemented with Buddhist and related texts written in Chinese but it is like that of the Pali in doctrine. Used by the Mahayana tradition primarily in China, Korea, Vietnam, and Japan.

'The Chinese produced the first woodblock edition of the Buddhist canon during the early Song Dynasty (972–83CE), and over the next thousand years, more than thirteen other editions were carved. These are considered invaluable treasures in both the Chinese cultural heritage and Buddhist literature. Although many scholars today use Taisho Canon printed in modern movable type, further research on the earlier woodblock editions will help us understand how the Chinese imperial court, Buddhist monks, and lay people managed such a huge printing project. The production of any edition of the Chinese Buddhist canon was a massive undertaking, requiring decades to...' (3-2).

Important elements of these canons have been preserved in Sanskrit and in Chinese translation. However, the Pali canon is the only one to have survived intact in its original Indian language. These texts, commonly referred to as the *Tipitaka*, form the scriptural basis of the southern tradition of Buddhism.

3. Tibetan Canon

The Tibetan Canon used in Indo–Tibetan Buddhism preserved many Buddhist texts that were originally composed in India. Most texts were translated from Sanskrit, Prakrit, and other Indic languages between the 7th and 14th centuries CE.

It consists of:

1. *Tengyur* (Translated Commentaries) by Indian and Tibetan scholars on Buddhist teachings. It includes works on logic,

medicine, arts, grammar, and philosophy, written by great Indian masters such as Nagarjuna, Vasubandhu, Asanga, and others. The *Tengyur* comprises around 225 volumes, depending on the edition. Additionally, it includes *sutras* (discourses) and *tantras* (esoteric teachings). The Tibetan Canon is organized into different sections, including the *Vinaya* (monastic discipline), *Sutras* (teachings on various topics), and *Abhidharma* (philosophical analysis). The Tibetan canon also includes a distinctive body of tantric writings of Indian origin. It includes yogic practices, rituals, meditations using sacred mantras, and visualizations. These set out practical methods for realizing the supreme goal described in the Mahayana scriptures. Tantric Buddhism is commonly understood to represent a third path of practice referred to as *Vajrayana*.

2. *Kangyu* which contains the words of the Buddha, consists of about 108 volumes, though the number can vary in different editions. One of its most significant aspects is the influence of Indian Buddhism, as it safeguards numerous Indian Buddhist scriptures that were lost in India after the decline of Buddhism there. Over time, different Tibetan monasteries compiled their own editions of the canon, leading to variations such as the Derge, Lhasa, Narthang, and Peking editions.

The most widely studied early Buddhist material are the first four Pali Nikayas – *Digha Nikaya* (containing long *suttas*), *Majjhima Nikaya* (containing *suttas* of middle length), *Samyutta Nikaya* (containing *suttas* organized according to content), *Anguttara*

Nikaya (containing numerical discourses). With these are the corresponding Chinese Agamas.

The Sthavira tradition emphasized adherence to what it saw as the original doctrines and stricter monastic discipline.

The Sthavira Nikaya schools split away from the majority Mahasamghikas during the Second Buddhist council. Modern scholarship is in opinion that the *Mahasamghikas Vinaya* is the oldest. The Sthavira divided into other schools such as: Sarvastivada and Vatsiputriya and Vibhajyavada.

Again, Vibhajyavada split into a number of schools such as Mahisasaka, Dharmaguptaka Kasyapiya and Tamraparni. The Theravada school of Sri Lanka and southeast Asia has identified itself exclusively with the Sthaviras. As Thera and Sthavira, both mean 'old', it is believed by the early Western historians to assume that the two groups are identical. But this is not true.

The major text apart from the *sutras* are the *Vinayas*. It is primarily concerned with aspects of the monastic discipline and the rules and procedures that govern the Buddhist monastic community or *sangha*. The *Vinaya* literature, in fact, contains discussion on the monastic rules, how they came about, how they developed, and how they were applied. But the *Vinaya* also contains some doctrinal expositions, ritual and liturgical texts, biographical stories, and some elements of the *Jatakas* or birth stories.

Various *Vinaya* collections are those of the following schools – Theravada in Pali, Mula-Sarvastivada in Tibetan translation and the Mahasanghika, Sarvastivada, Mahishasura, and Dharmaguptaka in Chinese translation. Besides that, there are a number of *Vinayas* that survived in various languages. The Dharmaguptaka is one of the eighteen or twenty early Buddhist schools, depending on the source. They are said to have originated from another sect, the Mahisasakas.

Abhidharma texts are a collection of Buddhist texts dating from 3 BCE onwards. They contain detailed scholastic presentations of doctrinal material appearing in the canonical Buddhist scriptures and commentaries.

There are two full canonical *Abhidharma* collections: the *Theravada Abhidhamma* and the *Sarvastivada Abhidharma*, that have survived. They both contain seven texts, which survive in Chinese translation. However, texts of other traditions, such as the *Sariputrabhidharma* of the Dharmaguptaka school, the *Tattva Siddhisstra* (Chengshilun), and various Abhidharma type works from the Pudgalavada school (3-3).

There are also some schools having minor or miscellaneous texts like *Khuddaka Nikaya* in the Theravada, the *Ksudraka Agama* in the Dharmaguptaka, etc. The Sarvastivada school also seems to have had a Ksudraka collection of texts.

Some other minor collections include, the Dhammapada, the Pali Udana, the Sarvastivada Udanavarga, the Pali Itivuttaka, the Pali *Sutta Nipata*, including texts such as the *Atthakatha* and *Parayanavagga*, *Theragatha* and *Therigatha,* two collections of verses, etc. There are also some unique individual texts like the *Milinda Panha* (The Questions of Milinda) and its parallel in Chinese, the *Nagasena Bhiksu Sutra.* These texts depict a dialogue between the monk Nagasena, and the Indo-Greek King Menander (Pali: Milinda). It is a compendium of doctrine, and covers a range of subjects.

Scholars like Buddhaghosa (5th century CE) and Dhammapala worked with the Theravada tradition in Sri Lanka. Buddhaghosa was also the author of the *Visuddhimagga* (Path of Purification). It is a manual of doctrine and practice written in accordance with the Mahavihara tradition of Sri Lanka. The manual systematizes the 5th century understanding and interpretation of the Buddhist path as maintained by the elders of the Mahavihara Monastery in Anuradhapura, Sri Lanka. Another work is the *Vimuttimagga* (Path of Freedom) which is a Buddhist practice manual, traditionally attributed to the *Arahant Upatissa*. It was translated into Chinese in the sixth century. Though the original text is no longer in existence, the work has survived in Chinese.

Another highly influential Pali Theravada work is the *Abhidhammattha-sangaha* (11th or 12th century) which is the Compendium of Things contained in the *Abhidhamma*. This Pali Buddhist instructional manual of the *Abhidhamma* of the Theravada tradition was written by the Sri Lankan monk Achariya Anuruddha sometime between the 8th century and the 12th century.

In Burmese Buddhist literature, the long and embellished translations of Pali Buddhist work in the form of poetry is found in which mainly *Jataka* stories are described.

HINAYANA AND MAHAYANA

Buddhism is divided into two great schools namely Hinayana and Mahayana. Both systems originated in India, but since Hinayana is confined almost exclusively to Ceylon, Burma, and Siam, while Mahayana predominates in China, Japan, Nepal, and, in a modified form, in Tibet and Mongolia. They are often, and rather incorrectly, known as Northern and Southern Buddhism.

Scholars of Buddhist studies such as Richard Gombrich, Akira Hirakawa, Alexander Wynne, and A. K. Warder believe that early

Buddhist texts contain material found possibly from the historical Buddha himself, or at least to the early years of pre-sectarian Buddhism. These texts are sometimes referred to as *Hinayana* or Srava Kalyana. Hinayana is the earlier and more primitive form of Buddhism.

In *Mahayana* Buddhism most of the early *sutras* that have survived are from *Sthavira Nikaya* (School of the Elders), one of the early Buddhist schools to emerge following the First Buddhist Council held shortly after the Buddha's death. This school later gave rise to several sub-schools, many of which preserved and developed distinct interpretations of the Buddha's teachings.

Mahayana is further divided into unreformed and reformed branches. The unreformed branch is found throughout east Asia, while the reformed branch is centred in Japan. Mahayana Buddhism is based principally upon the path of a bodhisattva. The name Mahayana means 'greater vehicle' that implies that these scriptures intend to describe a superior path. The ultimate aim of this spiritual practice is not the fulfilment of one's own nirvanic aspirations, which Mahayanists associated with the enlightenment realised by the arahat, but the complete and perfect awakening attained by the Buddha himself. This path is illustrated in Mahayana writings by the bodhisattva, who vows to work for the liberation of all beings. Some of these writings, known as the *Prajnaparamita Sutras* (Perfection of Wisdom *Sutras*), point to a more profound wisdom that can be attained through deep contemplation on the 'emptiness' of all things.

What Buddha and his subsequent followers had said orally are compiled in texts and during transmission and edit, the originality of the words Buddha and his immediate disciples said has not remained intact. They are changed sometimes to such an extent that the original words they rendered cannot be said to be their words and the faithful representation of Buddha. Scholars have raised this question. Luis Oscar Gomez Rodriguez, renowned for his extensive contributions to the study of particularly Mahayana Buddhism rightly said, 'Transmitted and edited through the oral tradition, the words of the Buddha and his immediate disciples had suffered many transformations before they came to be compiled, to say nothing of their state when they were eventually written down. We have no way of determining which, if any, of the words contained in the Buddhist scriptures are the words of the founder... Evidently, the Pali canon, like other Buddhist scriptures, is the creation, or at least the compilation and composition, of another age and a different linguistic milieu. As they are preserved today, the Buddhist scriptures must be a collective creation, the fruit of the effort of several generations of memorisers, redactors, and compilers.

'Many scholars in the history of the field have stressed the importance of considering more than written textual data. This has traditionally taken the form of advocating the study of epigraphy, art, ritual, culture, "Buddhist mentality", etc. , alongside, or as supplements to, textual material. E. Burnouf, arguably the father of Buddhist Studies, himself used epigraphical material to shed light on the meaning of the words and phrases in the texts he studied...' (3-4).

The influence of the canonical texts remains strong, especially in presentations of Buddhist philosophy. It is generally accepted that canonical texts are an important source for understanding how Buddhist thinkers in the early centuries of the CE framed their own philosophical inquiries. While there are disagreements on interpretations of the texts, the authority of the texts was never in question.

There is the heterogeneity of Buddhist Studies. It is evident not only at the institutional level but in other respects as well. In recent years the textual and philological ground upon which the discipline was implicitly based has been the subject of increasing critical scrutiny. There is some sort of perception that this heterogeneity has left the apparently once firm foundations of the discipline, if not teetering, at least in question (3-4).

'It may be inappropriate to call Buddhist Studies a discipline, especially if we take disciplines to be exemplified by such fields as history, anthropology, art history and so forth. Analogous to the Buddhist argument concerning the self and the aggregates, it might be contended that Buddhist Studies is not a discipline because it contains disciplines as parts. This, however, could simply be a question of historical evolution, for there was a time when even the classical disciplines did not seem particularly disciplinary-like. The fact that Buddhist Studies today seems the educated attention, interest and support of are in contention. Not to speak to these issues by retreating in reactionary, isolationist or sceptical ways is in effect to give up one's vote: to forsake the opportunity of allowing one's voice to be heard. The alternative, as I have mentioned, is to enter the methodological debate in a way that is both critical and dialogical. To do so is not only to accept the fact of methodological heterogeneity but also its implications. The different theoretical approaches to the study of Buddhism challenge each other and demand not only mutual respect but mutual response. Of course, such a dialogue must begin with an identification of the different perspectives. One of the best entrees into the identification of the variant styles of scholarship is not through their sympathetic depict (Pg 243, 3-5).'

However, it is undoubtedly to be admitted that the core teachings of Buddhism exhibit a coherence that compels us to see them as the work of a single mind. Without such admission, Buddhism could not be dealt with. As Étienne LaMotte, remarked, 'Buddhism could not be explained unless we accept that it has its origin in the strong personality of its founder' (3-5).

Gombrich explains: 'It should go without saying that we are not bound to take what a Pali text – or any other text in the world – says at face value. But our initial working hypothesis has to be that the text is telling the truth, and in each case where we do not believe it, or doubt it, we must produce our reasons for doing so. There will be innumerable such cases and all kinds of reasons' (3-6).

In short, Buddhism is a living tradition with its origins in the seminal teachings attributed to the historical Buddha and those teachings have always been the subject of interpretation and analysis.

4

THE ENLIGHTENED PHILOSOPHY OF BUDDHISM

The three core aspects of Buddhist philosophy are often summarised as the *Triratna* (Three Jewels). Buddhists take refuge in these three fundamental aspects:

- **Buddha** – The enlightened one who serves as a guide.
- **Dharma** – Buddha's teachings, which provide the path to liberation. These were orally transmitted for several centuries before being written down. Over time, different Buddhist traditions (Theravada, Mahayana, Vajrayana) interpreted and expanded the teachings in various ways some of which became complex due to philosophical developments, cultural influences, and commentaries by later scholars.
- ***Sangha*** – The *Sangha* are largely dealt with in the *Vinaya* Pitaka in its various versions. It is the community of those

who follow the Buddha's teachings. There are two types of '*Sangha*' in Buddhism.

The Monastic Sangha (*Bhikshu/Bhikshuni Sangha*)which consists of ordained monks (*bhikshus*) and nuns (*bhikshunis*) who dedicate their lives to practising the Dharma by following strict rules (*Vinaya*), renouncing worldly life, and focusing on meditation and ethical conduct. They have preserved Buddhist teachings and scriptures.

The Lay Sangha (Upasakas and Upasikas) includes householders who support the monastic community.

Buddhism is one of the great religions of the world. It is the world's fourth-largest religion, the followers of which are known as Buddhists. They comprise seven per cent of the global population. Buddhism originated in the eastern Gangetic plain as a Sramana–movement in the 5th century BCE, and gradually spread throughout much of Asia. It has subsequently played a major role in Asian culture and spirituality, eventually spreading to the West in the beginning of the 20th century.

Buddhism has its own distinctive features that enable it to be a class by itself. First, it is a lofty philosophy of humanism which is committed to the emancipation of the whole mankind. Secondly, it has made an unparalleled contribution to art, culture and literature. Thirdly, it encompasses a variety of meditation practices as a part of the path toward liberation from *kleshas* (defilements) and *upadana* (clinging and craving), also called awakening, which results in the attainment of nirvana. Last but not the least is its intellectual background that makes it much more than a religion.

The Buddha is the Enlightened or Awakened One. *Vinaya Pitaka* (Texts), the very first collections of dialogues Goutama Buddha preached to his first converts contains *Anatta Lakkhana Sutta* which is the discourse on the absence of any sign of soul in any of the constituent elements of individual life. All religions have mainly been founded on 'the belief in a divine power, acknowledgement of sin, the habit of prayer, the desire to offer sacrifice, and the hope of a future life' (4-1). But Buddhism has none of these.

Unlike other religions, Buddhism ignores the theory of God and the Soul. The origin of these two theories, however, is very little-known today. Primitive men have left no records. What ancient men anticipated came to stand as beliefs. Therefore, they cannot be regarded as authentic, and scholars differ on them.

Primitive men were down-to-earth people who did not look upon life as a dream. To them, life was a hard reality. Therefore, whatever they experienced everyday led them to form their own conclusions particularly about Nature and its phenomena. Again, whenever they had dreams, they thought them to be real. If, in one such dream, a man saw someone who was not alive, he would think that he was alive though his body had been destroyed. This made him think that there was something which couldn't be destroyed. Thus, came the idea of 'soul' which, as an inseparable part, remains integral to the body of a person while alive but when he dies, his body perishes but the 'soul' remains as it is when it leaves the dead. Though the 'soul' theory appeared in different ancient religious books in different ways, the basic idea remained more or less the same – the body of a person perishes but the soul is immortal. It wanders from one body to another. How the theory took this concrete shape is still a debatable point.

People believed that the soul was free and could move from one body to another. Like humans, animals were also thought to have souls. This idea of the soul came from mysterious natural events that early humans couldn't explain. Out of fear, they believed unseen spirits were behind these events. Powerful natural forces like fire, storms, floods, earthquakes, and volcanoes seemed beyond understanding, so they were seen as the work of evil spirits. As a result, many thought that trees, plants, seas, rivers, stars, the sun, the moon, and even the earth and sky were filled with ghostly spirits, though not everyone agreed with this view.

In early societies, deities were first introduced, and since these societies were female-centred, the earliest records mention goddesses, not gods. The concept of God emerged later, created by humans. Women were the leaders of ancient societies, and deities were born from them, leading to the idea of God. This idea was originally formed in the minds of devotees and, over time, evolved into the creation of more and more gods.

The ancient soul theory reached an advanced stage in the Vedic hymns. By studying the Rigveda and tracing the philosophical developments through the Upanishads up to the time of Buddha in 563 BCE, we see that Hindus were deeply engaged with questions about the individual soul (*atman*) and the universal soul (*Brahman*). Apart from the Jews, no other civilization was as intensely involved in exploring these spiritual concepts. This idea of religion has a systematic evolution and people of this continent held this religious belief for more than fifteen centuries before the birth of Jesus Christ, till the present time. In fact, India has a very authentic record of the above-mentioned period that is quite unlikely in other religious beliefs of the world, though God and belief in the soul are to be found in all the religious discussions of the world.

Buddhist philosophy combines both philosophical reasoning and the practice of meditation. It comprises all the philosophical investigations and systems of rational inquiry that developed among various schools of Buddhism in ancient India following the *parinirvana* of Gautama Buddha as well as the further developments which followed the spread of Buddhism throughout Asia.

First, we come across Pre-sectarian Buddhism or the earliest Buddhism or original Buddhism which is theorized to have existed around 250 BCE before the various Early Buddhist schools developed.

According to Buddhist tradition, the Buddha taught that attachment or clinging causes *dukkha* but that there is a path of development which leads to awakening and full liberation from *dukkha*. This path employs meditation practices and ethical precepts rooted in non-harming, with the Buddha regarding it as a Middle Way between extremes such as asceticism or sensual indulgence. The widely observed teachings include the Four Noble Truths, the Eightfold Noble Path, and the Doctrines of Dependent Origination, the Three Marks of Existence, and *Karma*. Other commonly observed elements include the taking of monastic vows and the cultivation of *paramita* (perfection).

Buddhist schools vary in their interpretation of the paths to liberation as well as the relative importance and canonicity assigned to various Buddhist texts, and their specific teachings and practices.

Particular points of Buddhist philosophy have often been the subject of disputes between different schools of Buddhism, as well as between representative thinkers of Buddhist schools and Hindu or Jain philosophers. These elaborations and disputes gave rise to various early Buddhist schools of Abhidharma, the Mahayana movement, and scholastic traditions. Early Buddhism is commonly divided into eighteen philosophical schools – including such influential traditions as *Sarvastivada*, *Vaibhasika*, *Sautrantika*, *Sthaviravada*, *Mahasaṃghika*, and so forth – though more are actually mentioned in Indic sources. Each of these developed its own distinctive philosophical system and engaged in debate with both Buddhist and non-Buddhist rivals. With the rise of Mahayana, new philosophical systems – including the Middle Way school (*Madhyamika*), the Yogic Practice school (*Yogacharya*), and the Epistemological school (*Pramana*) – developed. Tantric Buddhism added a new stream of philosophical thought that developed the conceptual implications of tantric scriptural texts.

One recurrent theme in Buddhist philosophy has been the desire to find a Middle Way between philosophical views seen as extreme (4-3).

Edward Conze splits the development of Indian Buddhist philosophy into three phases:

The first is the phase of the pre-sectarian Buddhist doctrines derived from oral traditions that originated during the life of Gautama Buddha, and are common to all later schools of Buddhism. The second phase concerns non-Mahayana scholastic Buddhism, as evident in the Abhidharma texts beginning in the 3rd century BCE. It features scholastic reworking and schematic classification of material in the early Buddhist texts. The *Abhidhamma* philosophy of the Theravada school belongs to this phase. The third phase concerns Mahayana Buddhism, beginning in the late first century CE. This movement emphasizes the path of a bodhisattva and includes various schools of thought, such as *Prajnaparamita*, *Madhyamaka*, *Sautrantika*, Buddha-nature, and *Yogacara*. The philosophy and worldview of various sects of Buddhism emerged from the incorporation of different kinds of elements of these three phases.

According to the Indian Buddhist philosophers, the teachings of Gautama Buddha were not meant to be taken on faith alone, but to be confirmed by logical analysis and *Pramana* (inquiry) of the world. The Buddha also expected his disciples to approach him as a teacher in a critical fashion and scrutinize his actions and words, as shown in the *Vimamsaka Sutta*.

The Vimamsaka *Sutta* (MN 47, The Inquirer) is the 47th discourse within Majjhima Nikaya of Pali Canon in Theravada Buddhism along with 'The discourse on investigating for the sake of understanding', (MA 186 T 26. 186) in the Madhyama Agama of the Chinese Taisho Tripitaka. As Bhikkhu Analayo says, it presents 'a remarkable advocacy of free inquiry' by making the Buddha's claim to awakening the object of 'the most searching scrutiny'.

The Buddha also encourages a monk to directly ask him about his mental states thus: 'Are there found in the *Tathagata* or not any defiled states cognizable through the eye or through the ear?'

Thus, a process of personal critical inquiry was indulged to increase one's faith and confidence in the Buddha and his teachings.

Once one gains a certain confidence in the Buddha and his teachings, he then put them into practice and verifies their effectiveness through direct personal experience which leads to confidence. If one has investigated and practised well, one's faith and confidence will be strong.

'*Bhikkhus*, when anyone's faith has been planted, rooted, and established in the *Tathagata* through these reasons, terms, and phrases, his faith is said to be supported by reasons, rooted in vision, firm; it is invincible by any recluse or brahmin or God or Mara or Brahma or by anyone in the world. That is how, *bhikkhus*, there is an investigation of the *Tathagata* in accordance with the Dhamma, and that is how the *Tathagata* is well-investigated in accordance with the Dhamma.'

In this way, an initial doubt about the Buddha and his dhamma is encouraged and seen as central to the growth of faith through evaluation and investigation of the teacher and their teachings.

5

FOUR MAJOR BUDDHIST COUNCILS

The fundamental doctrines of the Buddha and the great religious teachings he had imparted have continued to be transmitted during the last twenty-six centuries. Buddha's greatness consists not only in his attainment of nirvana but also in the fact that after the lapse of centuries, the nirvana that he had rendered has remained practicable for thousands of human beings. Over the period, Buddhist monastic communities have held conventions which are called Buddhist Councils. There they themselves recited together texts of scriptures, and approved them by settling up the Buddhist doctrinal disputes. In doing so, they have created a vast number of philosophical and literary works along with the development of a vast canonical literature. As a result, the Buddhist canon has not a unitary version but numerous. It has been constantly refined and evolved through conventions, various practices and councils.

There were four major Buddhist Councils that were held to discuss the ideas and philosophy of Buddhist doctrines and to refine and institutionalise them.

The first one was immediately held in Rajagriha (Rajgir, Bihar) immediately after the death of Buddha. Mahakasyapa, one of his senior disciples, convened the council where, it is learnt, 500 enlightened monks had taken part to determine how to go forward without their teacher. The convention was patronized by Ajatashatru of the Haryanka dynasty.

The First Council – the objectives were to preserve the *suttas* (Buddha's sayings) and the monastic discipline or rules which are included in *Vinaya*. The *Suttas* were recited by Ananda, and the *Vinaya* was recited by Upali. Even though the Buddha had said that the *Sangha* could abolish the minor rules after his passing, the council made the unanimous decision to keep all the rules intact.

There were disputes and disagreements that were found in numerous *Vinayas*. The Buddha while conversing had told Ananda that the minor rules might be abolished. This became the point of disagreements among different monks assembled there. It is learnt that Mahakasyapa criticized Ananda in various ways. Analayo quotes one passage from a Chinese parallel to *Mahaparinibbana-sutta* where Mahakassapa says: 'Ananda is (like) a lay person. I am afraid that, being with covetousness in his mind, he will not recite the discourses completely'. Analayo writes there may have been 'actual conflict between two contending factions in the monastic community after the Buddha's death, with the more aesthetically inclined faction emerging as the winning party in the accounts of the first *sangiti*' (5-2). Pete Harvey states that the assembled monks agreed to preserve the Buddha's teachings by memorizing and chanting them.'But while early generations of Buddhist monks and nuns probably did memorize and chant the Buddha's teachings, some historians question whether this First Buddhist Council actually took place (5-2).' According to Charles Prebish too, almost all scholars have questioned the historicity of this first council (5-1).

The Second Buddhist Council was held 100 years after the *parinirvana* of the Buddha in the Valukarama of Vaishali. It was patronized by the king Kalashoka (5-1). The monks assembled there did not agree on all points, especially that the *bhikkhus* at Vaishali known as Vajjiputtiya had been accepting monetary donations and following other lax practices. The Vajjiputtiya, one century after the Buddha's death, brought forward *dasa vatthuni* (Ten Points) as being permissible for members of the Order. These points are as follows:

1. *singilonakappa* or storing of salt in a horn.
2. *duvangulakappa* or eating of food when the shadow of the sun had passed two fingers' breadth beyond noon.
3. *gamantarakappa* or to eat once and then go again to the village for alms.
4. *avasakappa* or holding of the *uposatha* separately by monks dwelling in the same district.
5. *anumatikappa* or carrying out of an official act when the assembly is incomplete.
6. *acinnakappa* or following of a practice because it is so done by one's tutor or teacher.
7. *amathitakappa* or eating of sour milk by one who has already had his midday meal.
8. *jalogikappa* or use of strong drink before it has fermented.

9. *nisidanakappa* or use of a rug which is not of the proper size.
10. *jataruparajatakappa* or use of gold and silver.

The orthodox monks did not agree to these points. Yasa Kakandakaputta, one of the orthodox monks, publicly condemned the action of the Vajjiputtakas. Yasa then left Kosambi. He then, summoned monks from Pava in the west and Avanti in the south, sought Sambhuta Sanavasi in Ahoganga. Then they sought Soreyya-Revata, and together they consulted Sabakami at Valikarama and the Ten Points were declared invalid. The decision was conveyed to the monks. Soon after was held a recital of the Doctrine in which seven hundred monks took part under the leadership of Soreyya-Revata. The recital lasted eight months (5-3).

However, Mahasamghikas hold that the *Sthaviras* (Elders) wanted to add more rules to the *Vinaya*. *Vinaya* texts associated with the Sthaviras contain more rules than those of the *Mahasamghika Vinaya*. The *Mahasamghika Pratimoksa* (list of rules) has 67 rules in the *saiksa-dharma* section, while the Theravada version has 75 rules. The *Mahasamghika Vinaya* discusses how the Mahasamghika disagree with the Sthavira additions to the *Vinaya*.

From the Second Council emerged the two different schools of thought – Sthaviravadins and Mahasanghika. Sthaviravadins advocated strict adherence to the original tradition of Buddhism and compliance with the pure teachings of the Buddha while Mahasanghikas advocated a liberal attitude towards the rules prescribed in the Pitakas.

The Third Buddhist Council (247 BCE) was convened by Ashoka at the request of Venerable Moggaliputta Tissa in Pataliputra

(Patna), Emperor Ashoka's capital in which one thousand monks assembled. Emperor Ashoka himself attended the convention. Theravada sources contain narratives of the Third council of the Theravada school. It aimed primarily to eliminate corrupt practices of bogus monks from the *Sangha*. As it was patronised by Emperor Ashoka, a huge number of highly ambitious people flocked to the *Sangha* with their wrong views and tried to manipulate the order and bring divisions in the *Sangha*. Emperor Ashoka asked the suspect monks what the Buddha taught. They could not reply and what they replied had no relation with the Buddha.

The Theravadins say that the council recited the scriptures and added Moggaliputta Tissa's book, *Kathavatthu*, to the canon. This text, part of the Theravada *Abhidhamma* Pitaka, contrasts orthodox Theravada views with various dissenting Buddhist perspectives. The third council also likely led to the split between the Sarvastivada and Vibhajyavada schools. The approved teaching and philosophy of this Council is termed as Theravada. Ashoka sent Thera (elder) monks as representatives of Dhamma Mission to nine different countries for the spread of Dhamma. The Dhamma missions of these monks succeeded in spreading Buddhism abroad.

In this context elder monks or Thersa and their places of visit can be mentioned.

a. *Majjhantika Thera*: Kashmir and Gandhara region (Kashmir, Afghanistan, Northwest Pakistan)
b. *Mahadeva Thera*: Mahisha Mandala (Mysore)
c. *Rakkhita Thera*: Vanavasi (South India)

d. *Yonaka Dhamma Rakkitha Thera*: Aparantaka (Modern Northern Gujarat)
f. *Maha Dhamma Rakkitha Thera*: Maharattha (Parts of Maharashtra around the source of Godavari)
g. *Maha Rakkhita Thera*: Yonakaloka (Ancient Greece)
h. *Majjhima Thera*: Himavanta Padesa Bhaga (Himalayan region)
i. *Sona* and *Uttara Theras*: Suvanna Bhumi (Burma)
j. *Mahinda Thera*: Tambapanni Dipa (Sri Lanka)

The Fourth Buddhist Council was convened by Kanishka, in Kundalvana near Srinagar, Kashmir. At that time conflicting doctrines prevailed among various sects. Kaniska took help from the Venerable Parsva, who organized a general assembly of theologians in Kundalvana near Srinagar, Kashmir. All 500 members were from the Hinayana School. They elected Vasumitra the President, and Asvaghosa the Vice-president. Under their guidance they examined ancient theological literature and created detailed commentaries on the Canon's three main divisions. After the council, these commentaries were inscribed on copper sheets and stored in a *stupa* built by Kanishka.

However, the Fourth Council of Kashmir is not recognized as authoritative for the Theravadins. Reports of this council were kept in scriptures in the Mahayana tradition.

6

THE TRIPITAKA

The divisions and subdivisions among the sects took place continuously, and by the time of Ashoka, the *Sangha* had been divided and subdivided into eighteen sects (*Nikayas*). Most of the major sects compiled their own version of the Buddha-*vacana*. All sects unanimously accept that the corpus of the Buddha-*vacana* is grouped under *navanga* (nine limbs), under the heads – *sutra*, *geya*, *vyakarana*, *gatha*, *undana*, *iti vattaka*, *jataka*, *adbhuta dharma*, and *vedalla* (*vaipulya*).

Among all the sects of Buddhism, Sthaviravada is believed to be the most orthodox one and votaries of this sect claim to have in their possession the authentic teachings of the Buddha. Sthaviravada was transplanted in Sri Lanka by Mahinda and Sanghamitra the son and daughter of the Emperor Ashoka. It is known as Theravada which is a living religious tradition even today and there are millions of followers in countries such as Sri Lanka, Myanmar, Thailand, Kampuchea, and Laos. Theravada tradition has preserved their canon Tripitaka, recorded in the Pali (Magadhi) language. While discussing the Buddhist canon and its divisions, the Theravada Canon may be taken up first.

It is well-known that the Buddhist canon is traditionally called Tripitaka, which means three baskets. Tripitaka is, thus, is divided into three divisions - *Vinaya*, *Sutta* and *Abhidhamma.* Each basket (Tripitaka) was handed down from the teachers to the pupils from generation to generation from ancient times to today.

VINAYA PITAKA

The first of the three Pitakas is the Vinaya Pitaka, that deals with the Order of Mendicant Recluses. It lays down the rules to be followed by the male and female members of the *Sangha*. Thus, Vinaya Pitaka is mainly a guide to the mendicant monks. It has three divisions– i) *Sutta Vibhanga* ii) *Khandhakas* and, iii) *Parivara.*

i. *Sutta Vibhanga*

The first book of the *Vinaya* is the *Sutta Vibhanga* which means the exposition of rules. It has two parts – a) *Maha Vibhanga*, b) *Bhikkhuni Vibhanga*.

Sutta Vibhanga deals with each of the 227 rules in order in one particular method. It informs first how and when and why the particular rule in question came to be laid down. Then there is a literal commentary of the rules. Some rules are also interpreted with explanations to clear doubts.

The rules are divided into eight sections and at the end of each section the reciter asks the assembly whether it is blameless in respect thereof and receives the assurance that it is. If any member has offended, he has then and there to confess and receive absolution, or withdraw. The completion of the recitation is therefore evidence that all who have taken part in it are pure in respect of this specified offences. And this is the origin of that second name, the *Patimokkha* which means the acquittal or deliverance or discharge (6-1).

The general form of the commentary is that each rule is preceded by a story telling how the Buddha came to lay it down, and followed by explanations. Sometimes this includes further stories acting as judicial precedents.

FOUR PARAJIKAS

The Four Parajikas are the four most serious monastic rules in Theravada Buddhism, leading to permanent expulsion from the *Sangha* if violated.

The first rule prohibits sexual intercourse, requiring a monk to leave the order, though he may be reordained later in some traditions. However, in Sri Lanka, reordination is not permitted, and this rule does not allow nuns to return to monastic life after expulsion.

The second rule forbids stealing, including tax evasion, but compassionate actions such as releasing trapped animals are not considered violations.

The third rule prohibits killing a human being or encouraging suicide, with the *Sutta vibhanga* clarifying that abortion falls under this rule.

The fourth rule bans monks from falsely claiming spiritual attainments, such as enlightenment or supernatural powers, ensuring honesty and integrity within the monastic community. These rules uphold the discipline and ethical conduct essential for Buddhist monastic life.

THIRTEEN SANGHADISESA RULES

The Thirteen *Sanghadisesa* rules in Theravada Buddhism govern serious offenses that require formal probation and rehabilitation but do not result in expulsion. These rules are aimed at maintaining discipline among monks.

1. Deliberate sexual contact – engaging in physical contact with a woman out of lust, such as touching, holding hands, or embracing.
2. Arranging a date or sexual encounter – acting as a matchmaker or trying to set up a sexual encounter for oneself or another monk.
3. Speaking lustfully – making lewd or sexually suggestive comments to a woman.
4. Praising a woman's beauty to seduce her – complimenting a woman's appearance or virtues with the intention of arousing desire.
5. Making a false claim of spiritual attainment – lying about having reached enlightenment or possessing supernatural abilities.
6. Accusing an innocent monk of a parajika offense – falsely accusing another monk of a grave offense (such as sexual misconduct or murder) when it is untrue.
7. Creating a schism in the *sangha* – attempting to divide the monastic community by promoting conflict or dissent.
8. Persisting in controversial views that cause division – refusing to abandon a disruptive opinion that leads to disharmony within the *Sangha*.

9. Supporting a schismatic monk – siding with or following a monk who has been expelled for causing division.
10. Requesting and receiving luxurious monastic quarters improperly – asking for a grand dwelling and accepting it inappropriately (e. g. , built by laypeople with excessive effort).
11. Occupying luxurious monastic quarters improperly – living in such a place for more than three nights without inviting other monks to stay, violating the spirit of humility.
12. Criticising and refusing to accept correction – ignoring legitimate admonition from fellow monks regarding improper behaviour.
13. Giving unfair punishment – disciplining another monk unfairly or imposing a penalty without proper justification.

These offenses require formal correction, including probation, confession, and approval from a quorum of at least 20 monks before the offender is rehabilitated.

Besides the above rules, there are :

- *Aniyata* **(Two Rules)** – These deal with uncertain cases that might fall into different categories of offenses.
- *Nissaggiya Pacittiya* **(Thirty Rules)** – Violating these rules requires **expiation (confession)** and **forfeiture** of an improperly acquired or retained item. The forfeited item is returned to the monk after correction. The rule against accepting gold and silver (money) is absolute and does not allow for the item's return.
- *Pacittiya* **(Ninety-Two Rules)** – Breaching these rules requires **expiation (confession)** but no further penalty.

Some minor rules may be ignored, as per the **Suttavibhanga.**

- ***Patidesaniya*** **(Four Rules)** – Violations require **confession** before other monks.
- ***Sekhiya*** **(Seventy-Five Rules)** – These are **training rules**, mostly related to proper behaviour, etiquette, and manners.
- ***Adhikarana-samatha*** **(Seven Rules)** – These rules provide guidelines for **settling disputes** within the monastic community.

1. *Bhikkhuni Vibhanga*

The *Bhikkhuni Patimokkha* (rules for Buddhist nuns) has 311 rules. Out of these, 181 are the same as those for monks (*Bhikkhus*). These include:

- *Parajika* (4 major offenses)
- *Sanghadisesa* (7 serious rules)
- *Nissaggiya Pacittiya* (18 rules about giving up possessions)
- *Pacittiya* (70 minor offenses)
- *Sekhiya (*All 75 training rules)
- *Adhikarana-samatha* (All 7 rules for resolving disputes)

The rest of the rules are similar or related to rules for monks, including:

- 13 Pacittiya rules like those in the Khandhaka (monastic regulations)
- 1 Parajika rule like a monk's Sanghadisesa rule
- 1 Parajika rule like a monk's Pacittiya rule
- 2 Sanghadisesa-like rules similar to Khandhaka rules for monks

- 2 Nissaggiya Pacittiya like monks' NP rules
- 3 Pacittiya like monks' Sanghadisesa
- 7 Pacittiya like monks' Pacittiya
- 8 Pacittiya similar to monks' Khandhaka rules
- 8 Patidesaniya rules for nuns that expand on one monk's Pacittiya rule (6-2).

2. *Khandhaka*

The second book in the *Vinaya Pitaka* is *Khandhaka*. The term Khandaka refers to a section in the *Vinaya Pitaka*, specifically within the second book of the Theravada Buddhist canon which deals with various aspects of monastic life and administration, including rituals, ceremonies, ordination procedures, and disciplinary practices that are not covered in the more concise Patimokkha rules.

It has two volumes - a) *Mahavagga*, b) *Cullavagga*. Each collection contains several Khandakas, and each Khandaka focuses on a specific topic.

i. *Mahavagga*: It includes accounts of Gautama Buddha's and the ten principal disciples' awakenings, as well as rules for *uposatha* days and monastic ordination.
The *Mahavagga* has ten chapters:

a. The first chapter starts with a narrative beginning immediately after the Buddha's enlightenment and telling of the beginning of his preaching and foundation of the order of monks. It introduces rules on ordination and related matters.

b. The second chapter deals with the recitation of the Patimokkha, which is to take place every half month at new and full moons wherever there is a quorum of four monks.
c. The third is about the provision for the retreat for three months in the rainy season, when monks are to stay in one place except for specified reasons.
d. The fourth is about the invitation of the monks to their colleagues at the end of the retreat to know if they have any criticisms of their behaviours.
e. The fifth chapter deals with various topics.
f. The sixth chapter is on medicines. It has a passage which authorizes inhalation of smoke through a tube, which is used by some modern monks.
g. The seventh chapter called kathina – the process of making monastic robes – mainly deals with rule exemptions monks get after this process.
h. The eighth covers robe materials used by monks.
i. The ninth talks about a dispute among monks at Campa.
j. The tenth chapter describes a dispute that happened at Kosambi during the Buddha's time.

ii. Cullavagga: It includes accounts of the First and Second Buddhist councils and the establishment of the community of bhikkhunis, as well as rules for addressing offenses within the *sangha* (monastic community).

The Cullavagga has 12 chapters:

a. The first deals with various procedures to restrain badly behaved monks.
b. The second deals with probation for monks guilty of certain offenses.
c. The third deals with the case where a monk on probation commits a further offense.
d. The fourth chapter explains the seven rules for settling disputes.
e. The fifth chapter deals with minor matters.
f. The sixth is about lodgings.
g. The seventh chapter on schism tells the story of Devadatta, a cousin and disciple of the Buddha who sees the Buddha aging and suggests that the Buddha retire and let him take over leadership of the *Sangha*. When the Buddha refuses this proposal, Devadatta tries three times to kill him, but fails each time. After that, Devadatta proposes that the Buddha make monastic rules stricter, such as forcing monks to eat only vegetarian food, live in the forest only, wear robes made only from discarded cloth, etc. When the Buddha refuses to impose these strict rules on monks, Devadatta becomes angry and decides to form his own group of monks. This is called a schism, meaning a split or division in the *Sangha*.
h. The eighth chapter focuses on monastic discipline and the recitation of the Patimokkha, which is a regular confession ceremony held by monks. Normally, monks gather to recite the Patimokkha, which is a list of rules they follow. A monk can suspend the recitation if he knows that another monk has committed an offense

but hasn't confessed it. This suspension acts as a reminder and a prompt for that monk to confess and clear the matter before the community can continue.

i. The ninth chapter deals with nuns. The Buddha first refuses to establish an order of nuns but finally agrees to establish it. He, at the same time, warns that it will weaken the teaching and shorten its lifetime. He imposes some rules for organizing nuns' orders. It can be found in the Pali Canon, most notably the *Kunala Jataka*.
j. The tenth is about when shortly after the Buddha's death, Kassapa holds a council at which the teachings are recited; Upali answers questions on the *Vinaya* and Ananda on the dhamma.
k. The eleventh chapter is about when a century later a dispute arises on various points, mainly on the acceptance of gold and silver, another council is held which agrees on the stricter position, after receiving advice from an aged pupil of Ananda (6-3).

3. Parivara

Parivara, the meaning in Pali is Accessory or Appendix or Index is the third and last book of the Theravada *Vinaya Pitaka*. It is a summary form of the various rules identified in the *Vinaya Pitaka's* first two books. It is intended to assimilate the contents in the Suttavibhanga and the Khandhakas, primarily for didactic purposes. According to some scholars, it may be even later than the Fourth Council in Ceylon in the last century BCE, at which the Pali Canon was written down from oral tradition (6-4).

The Parivara acts as a *Vinaya* textbook for monks in training, and ensures proper application of rules. It also helps monks memorise, understand, and reflect on the disciplinary code. Lastly, it supports legal integrity of monastic acts.

The book contains 19 chapters:

1. *Matika* – A list of categories and key terms from the *Vinaya*, serving as an index or roadmap for the entire text on the rules of the monks.
2. *Mulapariyaya* – Arranges the rules in different patterns to help memorization, including groupings by number, theme, or rule type.
3. *Ubhatovibhaṅga Vibhanga* – presents a verse summary explaining the different ways an action can originate, especially in relation to the monastic rules (Patimokkha) for monks and nuns. It states that an action can arise either through the body or through speech. Each of these can be done either with intention or without intention. This results in six possible origins of an action: bodily action with intention, bodily action without intention, verbal (speech) action with intention, speech action without intention, combined body and speech action with intention, combined body and speech without intention. The chapter then systematically goes through all the Patimokkha rules and indicates which of these six types of actions can lead to a breach of each specific rule. In doing so, it highlights the importance of both the method and the intention behind an action when evaluating whether a monastic rule has been broken.
4. *Sikkhapada Vibhanga* – focusing on the origins of monastic offenses. It aims to clarify how actions arise and which

types of actions lead to a breach of specific rules in the Patimokkha (the core disciplinary code for monks and nuns). It explores the ethical and psychological roots of actions, reinforcing the Buddhist emphasis on intentionality and mindfulness in all aspects of life.

5. *Vinayadhara Vibhanga* – identifies legal cases and which dispute-settlement methods are applicable to each. Reviews and repeats classifications of legal cases (such as disputes, accusations, confessions) in the context of monastic discipline.
6. *Adhikaranavibhanga* – Further classification and detailed study of legal cases (offenses, disputes, accusations, etc.) and their resolution. Identifies which of the seven methods for resolving disputes (sattadhikarana-samatha) apply to different kinds of legal problems within the *Sangha*.
7. *Suttavibhanga-pariyatti* – Quiz-style or analytical questions and answers on the Khandhakas (the second book of the *Vinaya*), which deal with monastic procedures and community life to ensure monks understand the rules, their sources, and reasoning.
8. *Saratthadipani* – Details when a monk must suspend the **Patimokkha recitation** due to unresolved offenses or disputes. It presents a numerical classification of rules and concepts, helping monks remember them easily. It is inspired by the *Anguttara Nikaya*, a *sutta* collection organized by numbers.
9. *Kammavaca Vibhanga* – Explains how to correctly perform **formal acts of the *Sangha*** (ordination, penance, expulsion), and when they are invalid. This chapter ensures that

disciplinary and administrative acts within the *Sangha* are consistent, legally sound, and in line with the Buddha's prescriptions. It is especially valuable for senior monks and *Vinaya* teachers responsible for guiding the community through complex decisions and actions.

10. *Vinaya-katha* – Summarized discussions and questions and answers sessions about *Vinaya* topics, encouraging understanding through dialogue.

Chapters 11 to 19 of the *Parivara* form the final analytical and reflective portion of the text. These chapters are diverse in style – some are in verse, some are numerical lists, and some are practical guides – and they aim to deepen understanding, enhance memory, train monks in resolving disputes and performing duties properly. They deepen the *Vinaya* understanding through repetition, questioning, and case analysis. They emphasize practical application in resolving conflicts, performing ceremonies, and correcting behaviour.

2. *SUTTA* PITAKA

The next division is the *Sutta* Pitaka or the basket of discourses which was first orally rehearsed by Buddha's cousin Ananda at the First Buddhist Council that was held shortly after the Buddha's death which later it came as a written scripture.

Suttas from the *Sutta* Pitaka of the Pali Canon consists of more than 10,000 *suttas* (discourses) delivered by the Buddha and his close disciples during and shortly after the Buddha's forty-five-year teaching career, as well as many additional verses by other members of the *Sangha*. They are of five categories:

a. *Digha Nikaya Suttas*
b. *Majjhima Nikaya Suttas*
c. *Samyutta Nikaya Suttas*
d. *Anguttara Nikaya Suttas*
e. *Khuddaka Nikaya Suttas*

a. *Digha Nikaya Suttas*

The *Digha Nikaya Suttas* is the collection of long discourses and it is a collection of Buddhist scriptures. The subject matter of these *suttas* ranges widely, from colourful folkloric accounts of the beings inhabiting the deva worlds to down-to-earth practical meditation instructions, and everything in between. It was observed that the Digha Nikaya was intended for the purpose of propaganda, to attract converts to the new religion.

The Digha Nikaya consists of 34 discourses, divided into three groups:

1. *Silakkhandha-vagga – The Division Concerning Morality* (*Suttas* 1–13), named after a tract on monks' morality that appears in each *sutta*. In theory, this section includes a full account of morality, but in practice, it is not always written out in full. Most of these discourses proceed to describe the *jhanas* (meditative absorptions central to *samatha* meditation), the cultivation of psychic powers, and the attainment of the fruit of arahantship.
2. *Maha-vagga* – The Great Division (*Suttas* 14–23), consisting of 10 *suttas*.
3. *Patika-vagga* – The Patika Division (*Suttas* 24–34), consisting of 11 *suttas*.

b. *Majjhima Nikaya Suttas*

Composed between the 3rd century BCE and 2nd century CE, the Majjhima Nikaya is the Collection of Middle-length Discourses. It is the second collection in the *Sutta Pitaka* of the Pali Canon. It contains 152 discourses (*suttas*) attributed to the Buddha and his close disciples.

These discourses are called middle-length because they are not as long as those in the Digha Nikaya (Long Discourses), nor as short as those in the Samyutta or Anguttara Nikaya. They offer a balanced and detailed view of the Buddha's teachings.

The 152 *suttas* are grouped into three main parts, each with 50 or so *suttas*.

1. *Mulapannasa* (The First Fifty) focuses on foundational teachings like ethics, meditation, and mindfulness. It includes famous *suttas* like *Satipatthana Sutta* (Foundations of Mindfulness) and *Sabbasava Sutta* (All the Taints).
2. *Majjhimapannasa* (The Middle Fifty) discusses more refined psychological and philosophical teachings. It includes *Culamalunkya Sutta* (On unanswered questions) and *Alagaddupama Sutta* (The Simile of the Snake).
3. *Uparipannasa* (The Final Fifty-Two) deals with deep doctrinal issues like dependent origination, non-self, and ultimate liberation. It includes *Anattalakkhana Sutta* (The Discourse on Non-Self) and *Mahapunnama Sutta* (The Greater Discourse on the Full Moon).

The key *suttas* are:

1. *Mulapariyaya Sutta* – The Buddha listed clinging to views as one of the four forms of clinging that tie the mind to the processes of suffering. He thus recommended that his followers relinquish their clinging even in their rudimentary form (6-8).
2. *Sabbasava Sutta* – Discourse on All *Asavas* (Fermentations). Here the Buddha teaches seven methods for eliminating from the mind the deeply rooted defilements (sensuality, becoming, views, and ignorance) that obstruct the realisation of Awakening.
3. *Bhaya-bherava Sutta* – The *sutta* deals with fear and terror. What would it take to live in solitude in the wilderness, completely free of fear? The Buddha explains.
4. *Anangana Sutta* – Venerable Sariputta explains the blemishes of the mind, and the influences of evil, unskilful wishes.
5. *Akankheyya Sutta* – If One Would Wish. The wishes that can be fulfilled by bringing the precepts to perfection, being committed to inner tranquillity of awareness, not neglecting *jhana*, being endowed with insight, and frequenting empty dwellings.
6. *Vatthupama Sutta* – The Simile of the Cloth. With a simple simile the Buddha illustrates the difference between a defiled mind and a pure mind.
7. *Sallekha Sutta* – The Discourse on Effacement. The Buddha explains how unskilful qualities in the heart can be eradicated through meditation.
8. *Sammaditthi Sutta* – The Discourse on Right View. How the four noble truths, dependent co-arising, and the knowledge

that ends mental fermentation all build upon the basic dichotomy between skillful and unskilful action.

9. *Satipatthana Sutta* – The Establishing of Mindfulness Discourse. This *sutta* sets out the full formula for the practice of establishing mindfulness, and then gives an extensive account of one phrase in the formula – what it means to remain focused on any of the four frames of reference – body, feelings, mind, and mental qualities – in and of itself. (The text of this *sutta* is identical to that of the *Maha-Satipatthana Sutta*, but without its detailed exposition of the Four Noble Truths).
10. *Cula-sihanada Sutta* – The Shorter Discourse on the Lion's Roar. The Buddha declares that only through practicing in accord with the Dhamma can Awakening be realised. His teaching is distinguished from those of other religions and philosophies through its unique rejection of all doctrines of self.
11. *Maha-sihanada Sutta* – The Great Discourse on the Lion's Roar. The Buddha expounds the ten powers of a *Tathagata*, his four kinds of intrepidity, and other superior qualities which entitle him to 'roar his lion's roar in the assemblies'.
12. *Maha-dukkhakkhandha Sutta* – The Great Mass of Stress. In deliciously graphic terms, the Buddha describes the allures and drawbacks of sensuality, physical form, and feeling. What better incentive could there be to escape *samsara* once and for all?
13. *Cula-dukkhakkhandha Sutta* – The Lesser Mass of Stress. What mental qualities must be abandoned in order to free oneself of greed, aversion, and delusion? Can painful austerities be used to purify oneself and burn away the

karmic fruit of past misdeeds? Through question-and-answer dialogues with the lay follower Mahanama, and with a group of Jain ascetics, the Buddha lays these questions to rest.

14. *Madhupindika Sutta* – The Ball of Honey. A man looking to pick a fight asks the Buddha to explain his doctrine. The Buddha's answer mystifies not only the man, but also a number of monks. Venerable Maha Kaccana finally provides an explanation, and in the course of doing so explains what is needed to bring the psychological sources of conflict to an end.
15. *Dvedhavitakka Sutta* – Two Sorts of Thinking. The Buddha recounts the events leading up to his Awakening, and describes his discovery that thoughts connected with sensuality, ill-will, and harmfulness do not lead one to Awakening, while those connected with their opposites (renunciation, non-ill-will, and harmlessness) do.
16. *Vitakkasanthana Sutta* – The Removal of Distracting Thoughts/The Relaxation of Thoughts. The Buddha offers five practical methods of responding wisely to unskilful thoughts (thoughts connected with desire, aversion, or delusion).
17. *Kakacupama Sutta* – The Parable of the Saw/The Simile of the Saw. The Buddha tells the story of a wise slave who deliberately tests the mistress's patience. The Buddha invokes several memorable similes here to illustrate the correct way to develop patience.
18. *Alagaddupama Sutta* – The Snake Simile/The Water-Snake Simile. Using two famous similes, the Buddha shows how the development of the right view calls for the skillful

application both of grasping and of letting-go. The *sutta* includes one of the Canon's most important expositions on the topic of not-self.

19. *Ratha-vinita Sutta* – Relay Chariots. Using the simile of a set of relay chariots, Venerable Punna Mantaniputta explains the relationship of the factors of the path to the goal of the holy life.
20. *Ariyapariyesana Sutta* – The Noble Search. Most of us spend a good part of our lives looking for happiness in all the wrong places. In this *sutta* the Buddha recounts the story of his own search and points out where a true and lasting happiness can be found.
21. *Cula-hatthipadopama Sutta* – The Shorter Elephant Footprint Simile. At what point do you know for sure that the Buddha's awakening was genuine?
28. *Maha-hatthipadopama Sutta* – The Great Elephant Footprint Simile. An explanation of the four noble truths, focusing on the aggregate of physical form and showing (1) how all the aggregates are interrelated, and, (2) how all four noble truths, together with the principle of dependent co-arising, are related to the aggregates.
29. *Maha Saropama Sutta* – The Longer Heartwood-simile Discourse. The Buddha compares the rewards of the practice to different parts of a large tree, with total release of the most valuable part of the tree: the heartwood.
30. *Cula Saropama Sutta* – The Shorter Heartwood-simile Discourse. The Buddha compares the rewards of the practice to different parts of a large tree.

33. *Maha-gopalaka Sutta* – The Greater Cowherd Discourse. Eleven factors that are conducive to spiritual growth, and eleven that are obstructive.
34. *Culagopalika Sutta* – The Shorter Discourse on the Cowherd. In this brief excerpt the Buddha urges his monks to cross over to the lasting safety of *Nibbana*.
35. *Cula-Saccaka Sutta* – The Shorter Discourse to *Saccaka*. Even though the Buddha did not usually seek debates, he knew how to reply effectively when attacked. In this discourse, he gets *Saccaka* – who uses a variety of cheap debater's tricks – to trip over those tricks. However, the Buddha goes beyond simply defeating *Saccaka* in debate. He then takes the opportunity to teach him the Dhamma.
36. *Maha-Saccaka Sutta* – The Longer Discourse to *Saccaka*. In response to an insinuating remark – that his ability not to be overcome by pleasure and pain is due simply to the fact that he never experienced any intense pleasures or pains – the Buddha recounts the pains he endured in his austerities, and the pleasures that attended the path to and his attainment of Awakening.
38. *Mahatanhasankhaya Sutta* – The Greater Craving-Destruction Discourse. A long discourse in which the Buddha discusses how to understand the role of consciousness – as a process – in the process of birth in a way that actually can lead to the end of birth.
39. *Maha-Assapura Sutta* – The Greater Discourse at Assapura. The Buddha outlines the full course of training by which a meditator may earn the right to call themselves a true contemplative. As presented here, the training begins with

conscience and concern for the results of one's actions, and leads progressively through the cultivation of virtue, sense-restraint, moderation, wakefulness, mindfulness, alertness, the four *jhanas*, finally culminating in the realisation of the insight knowledges.

41. *Saleyyaka Sutta* – The Brahmans of Sala. A discussion of ten types of skilful and unskilful conduct in body, speech, and mind, and of the future rewards open to those who follow the guidelines to skilful conduct.

43. *Mahavedalla Sutta* – The Greater Set of Questions-and-Answers. Venerable Sariputta answers questions dealing with discernment, right view, and the higher meditative attainments.

44. *Culavedalla Sutta* – The Shorter Set of Questions-and-Answers. Dhammadinna the nun fields a series of Dhamma questions put to her by her former husband; questions on self-identification, cessation, penetration into the true nature of feeling, and the attainment of *Nibbana*.

45. *Cula-dhammasamadana Sutta* – The Shorter Discourse on Taking on Practices. Is something right because it feels right?

48. *Kosambiya Sutta* – In Kosambi. Teaching a group of monks who have been quarrelling over a minor matter, the Buddha outlines the causes for harmony in a group and reminds the monks of the purpose of their training – the right ending of suffering and stress.

49. *Brahma-nimantanika Sutta* – The Brahma Invitation. The Buddha disarms two powerful antagonists through his profound understanding of the nature of consciousness.

52. *Atthakanagara Sutta* – To the Man from Atthakanagara. Venerable Ananda describes eleven modes of practice that can lead to the Deathless.
53. *Sekha-patipada Sutta* – The Practice for One in Training. Consummate in clear-knowing and conduct is a standard epithet for the Buddha. This *sutta* explains what it means, and shows that it can be used to describe an *arahant* as well.
54. *Potaliya Sutta* – To Potaliya. Using seven graphic similes for the drawbacks of sensual passions, the Buddha teaches Potaliya the householder what it means, in the discipline of a noble one, to have entirely cut off one's worldly affairs.
57. *Kukkuravatika Sutta* – The Dog-duty Ascetic. Act like a dog, and that's what you'll become. The moral – choose your actions with care.
58. *Abhaya Sutta* – To Prince Abhaya. The Buddha explains the criteria for determining whether or not something is worth saying. This discourse is a beautiful example of the Buddha's skill as teacher. Not only does he talk about right speech, but he also demonstrates right speech in action.
59. *Bahuvedaniya Sutta* – The Many Kinds of Feeling/ Things to be Experienced. The Buddha discusses the range of possible pleasures and joys, and concludes by advocating a pleasure that goes beyond feeling.
60. *Apannaka Sutta* – A Safe Bet. The Buddha explains to a group of householders how to navigate skilfully through the maze of wrong views.
61. *Ambalatthika-rahulovada Sutta* – Instructions to Rahul at Mango Stone. The Buddha admonishes his son, the novice

Rahul, on the dangers of lying and stresses the importance of constant reflection on one's motives. This is one of the *suttas* selected by King Asoka (270-232 BCE) to be studied and reflected upon frequently by all practicing Buddhists. (See That the True Dhamma Might Last a Long Time: Readings Selected by King Asoka, by Thanissaro Bhikkhu.)

62. *Maha-Rahulovada Sutta* – The Greater Exhortation to Rahul. The Buddha delivers meditation instructions to his son, the novice Rahul.
63. *Cula-Malunkyovada Sutta* – The Shorter Instructions to Malunkya. Venerable Malunkyaputta threatens to disrobe unless the Buddha answers all his speculative metaphysical questions. Using the famous simile of a man shot by a poison arrow, the Buddha reminds him that some questions are simply not worth asking.
66. *Latukikopama Sutta* – The Quail Simile. Fetters are strong, not because of their own tensile strength, but because of the tenacity of our unwillingness to let them go.
70. *Kitagiri Sutta* – At Kitagiri. A discourse on the importance of conviction in the Buddhist path. Not only is conviction a prerequisite for listening to the Buddha's teachings with respect, but – as is shown by the unusual discussion here categorizing the types of noble disciples – it can underlie the practice all the way to the Deathless.
72. *Aggi-Vacchagotta Sutta* – To Vacchagotta on Fire. The Buddha explains to a wanderer why he does not hold any speculative views. Using the simile of an extinguished fire he illustrates the destiny of the liberated being.
74. *Dighanaka Sutta* – A discussion of how to abandon

doctrinaire views of radical acceptance, radical rejection, and any combination of the two.

75. *Magandiya Sutta* – The Buddha teaches a member of a hedonist sect about the nature of true pleasure and true health.
78. *Samana-Mundika Sutta* – *Mundika* the Contemplative. The highest attainment is not simply the abandoning of unskilful actions and a reversion to childlike harmlessness. It requires first developing skillful habits and skillful resolves, and then letting them go.
82. *Ratthapala Sutta* – About Ratthapala. A two-part story about the monk who, the Buddha said, was foremost among his disciples in ordaining on the power of pure conviction. In the first part of the story, Ratthapala deals with his parents' opposition to his ordaining, and their attempts, after ordination, to lure him back to lay life. In the second part, he recalls the four observations about the world that inspired him as a healthy and wealthy young man, to ordain in the first place.
86. *Angulimala Sutta* – About Angulimala. A murderous bandit takes refuge in the Buddha, develops a heart of compassion, and becomes an *arahant*.
87. *Piyajatika Sutta* – From One Who is Dear. King Pasenadi of Kosala figures prominently in many discourses as a devout follower of the Buddha. In this discourse we learn how – thanks to Queen Mallika's astuteness – the King first became favourably disposed toward the Buddha.
90. *Kannakatthala Sutta* – At Kannakatthala. A case study in how social advantages can be a spiritual liability. The discussion focuses on the factors needed for release –

attainable by all people, regardless of caste or race – while the gently satirical story shows how the life of a king, or any highly placed person, presents obstacles to developing those factors.

93. *Assalayana Sutta* – With Assalayana. The Buddha enters into a debate with a brahmin on whether one's worth as a person is determined by birth or by behaviour. Although some of the arguments he presents here deal with the specifics of brahman caste pride, many of them are applicable to issues of racism and nationalism in general.

95. *Canki Sutta* – A pompous brahman teenager questions the Buddha about safeguarding, awakening to, and attaining the truth. In the course of his answer, the Buddha describes the criteria for choosing a reliable teacher and how best to learn from such a person.

97. *Dhananjanin Sutta* – To Dhananjanin. A poignant story of a lay person whose welfare was of special concern to Venerable Sariputta, this discourse teaches two lessons in heedfulness.

    i. If you're engaging in wrong livelihood, don't expect to escape the karmic consequences even if you're doing it to fulfil your duties to your family, parents, or friends.
    ii. Don't be satisfied with mundane levels of attainment in meditation when there is still more to be done.

101. *Devadaha Sutta* – At Devadaha. The Buddha refutes a Jain theory of *kamma*, which claims that one's present experience is determined solely by one's actions in past lives, and that the effects of past unskilful actions can be

'burned away' through austerity practices. The Buddha here outlines one of his most important teachings on *kamma*: that it is both the results of past deeds and present actions that shape one's experience of the present. It is precisely this interaction of present and past that opens up the very possibility of Awakening.

102. *Pancattaya Sutta* – This discusses views that can get in the way of awakening. Some of the views are speculative, whereas as the most subtle obstruct. Buddha explains how he tames his disciples.
103. *Sunakkhatta Sutta* – The Buddha addresses the problem of meditators who overestimate their progress in meditation. The *sutta* ends with a warning – anyone who claims enlightenment as license for unrestrained behaviour is like someone who fails to follow the doctor's orders after surgery, who knowingly drinks a cup of poison, or who deliberately extends a hand toward a deadly snake.
104. *Anenja-sappaya Sutta* – Conducive to the Imperturbable. Advanced meditation instruction: how the fourth *jhana* and the formless attainments can be developed and used as a basis for the realisation of *Nibbana*.
105. *Ganaka Moggallana Sutta* – The Discourse to Ganaka-Moggallana. The Buddha sets forth the gradual training of the Buddhist monk and describes himself as a 'shower of the way'.
106. *Gopaka Moggallana Sutta* – Moggallana the Guardsman. Venerable Ananda explains how the *Sangha* maintains its unity and internal discipline after the passing away of the Buddha. Interestingly, this *sutta* also shows that early Buddhist practice had no room for many practices that

developed in later Buddhist traditions, such as appointed lineage holders, elected ecclesiastical heads, or the use of mental defilements as a basis for concentration practice.

107. *Maha-punnama Sutta* – The Great Full-moon Night Discourse. A thorough discussion of issues related to the five aggregates. Toward the end of the discussion, a monk thinks that he has found a loophole in the teaching. The way the Buddha handles this incident shows the proper use of the teachings on the aggregates not as a metaphysical theory but as a tool for questioning, clinging and so gaining release.
108. *Cula-punnama Sutta* – The Shorter Discourse on the Full-moon Night. How to recognize – and become – a person of integrity.
109. *Anupada Sutta* – One After Another. A description of how insight can be developed either while in, or immediately after withdrawing from, the different levels of *jhana*.
110. *Sappurisa Sutta* – A Person of Integrity. Who is a person of integrity?
111. *Isigili Sutta* – The Discourse at Isigili (Piyadassi). The Buddha enumerates the many Pacceka buddhas who lived on the Isigili mountain.
112. *Maha-cattarisaka Sutta* – The Great Forty. On the nature of noble right concentration, and its interdependence with all the factors of the noble eightfold path.
113. *Anapanasati Sutta* – Mindfulness of Breathing. One of the most important texts for beginning and veteran meditators alike, this *sutta* is the Buddha's roadmap to the entire course of meditation practice, using the vehicle of breath meditation. The simple practice of mindfulness of

breathing leads the practitioner gradually through sixteen successive phases of development, culminating in full Awakening.

114. *Kayagata-sati Sutta* – Mindfulness Immersed in the Body. This *sutta* serves as a companion to the Anapanasati *Sutta*, and explains the importance of establishing a broad awareness of the body in meditation to develop *jhana*.
115. *Cula-sunnata Sutta* – The Lesser Discourse on Emptiness (*Thanissaro*). The Buddha instructs Venerable Ananda on the practice that leads to the 'entry into emptiness' which is the doorway to liberation.
116. *Maha-sunnata Sutta* – The Greater Discourse on Emptiness (*Thanissaro*). The Buddha instructs Ananda on several practical aspects of the meditative dwelling in emptiness, a mode of awareness that can ultimately bring the meditator to the threshold of Awakening.
117. *Acchariyabbhutadhamma Sutta* – Amazing & Astounding Qualities (*Thanissaro*). A miraculous account of the Buddha's birth.
118. *Dantabhumi Sutta* – The Discourse on the 'Tamed Stage' (Horner). By analogy with the taming of an elephant, the Buddha explains how he tames his disciples.
119. *Bhumija Sutta* – To Bhumija (*Thanissaro*). Does the desire for Awakening get in the way of Awakening? According to this discourse, the question of desiring or not desiring is irrelevant as long as one develops the appropriate qualities that constitute the path to Awakening. The discourse is also very clear on the point that there are right and wrong paths of practice: as a geographer might say, not every river flows to the sea.

121. *Devaduta Sutta* – The Deva Messengers. The Buddha's eyewitness account of hell.

122. *Bhaddekaratta Sutta* – The Discourse on the Ideal Lover of Solitude/An Auspicious Day. In this stirring discourse the Buddha underscores the vital urgency of keeping one's attention firmly rooted in the present moment. After all, the past is gone, the future isn't here; this present moment is all we have.

123. *Cula-kammavibhanga Sutta* – The Shorter Exposition of *Kamma*/The Shorter Analysis of Action. Why do some people live a long life, but others die young? Why are some people born poor, but others born rich? The Buddha explains how *kamma* accounts for a person's fortune or misfortune.

124. *Maha Kammavibhanga Sutta* – The Great Exposition of *Kamma*/The Greater Analysis of Action (Nanamoli/ *Thanissaro*). Two lessons in the dangers of quick generalization. In the first, the Buddha points out that the perception of all feeling as stressful is not appropriate at all stages of the practice. In the second, he shows that generalising too quickly on the basis of what one sees in meditation can lead to serious wrong view.

125. *Salayatana-vibhanga Sutta* – An Analysis of the Six Sense-media (*Thanissaro*). A discussion of the emotions – where they come from, how they function in the path of practice, and how they manifest in an awakened person who is fit to teach others.

126. *Uddesa-vibhanga Sutta* – An Analysis of the Statement (*Thanissaro*). How to attend to outside objects without letting the mind become externally scattered, and how

to focus in strong states of absorption without becoming internally positioned. It's not easy, but it can be done.

127. *Dhatu-Vibhanga Sutta* – An Analysis of the Properties (*Thanissaro*). A poignant story in which a wanderer, searching for the Buddha, meets the Buddha without realising it. He recognizes his mistake only after the Buddha teaches him a profound discourse on four determinations and the six properties of experience. An excellent illustration of the Buddha's statement, 'Whoever sees the Dhamma sees me'.
128. *Saccavibhanga Sutta* – Discourse on the Analysis of the Truths/an Analysis of the Truths. Venerable Sariputta gives a detailed elaboration on the Buddha's teaching of the Four Noble Truths.
129. *Anathapindikovada Sutta* – Instructions to Anathapindika/ Advice to A Dying Man. Venerable Sariputta offers a deep teaching on non-clinging to the ailing lay-follower Anathapindika.
130. *Nandakovada Sutta* – Nandaka's Exhortation. Venerable Nandaka discusses impermanence with a large group of nuns, driving his point home with particularly vivid similes. It was an effective teaching. Soon afterwards, these nuns all became enlightened.
131. *Cula-Rahulovada Sutta* – The Shorter Exposition to Rahula (M iii 277). The Buddha leads his son, Venerable Rahula, to Arhantship.
132. *Chachakka Sutta* – The Six Sextets (*Thanissaro*). How the contemplation of the six senses leads to an understanding of not-self and, ultimately, to Awakening.

133. *Maha-salayatanika Sutta* – The Great Six Sense-media Discourse. How a clear understanding of the six senses leads to the development of the Wings to Awakening and to final release.
134. *Indriya-bhavana Sutta* – The Development of the Faculties. What qualifies as full mastery of the sermon (6-9).

c. *Samyutta Nikaya Suttas*

Pali Samyutta means group or 'collection'. The total number of *sutras* is unclear. The *sutras* are grouped into five *Vargas*, or sections. Each *Varga* is further divided into Samyuktha, or chapters. Each chapter contains a group of *sutras* on a related topic.

The Samyutta Nikaya corresponds to the Samyukta Agama. This is found in the *Sutra Pitikas* of various Sanskritic early Buddhists schools. It is divided into five divisions:

i. *Sagatha-varga* (Chapter with Verses) – Includes *suttas* with verses, often dialogues with devas (gods), kings, and other beings.
ii. *Nidana-varga* (Causal Chapter) – Explores the principle of dependent origination (*Paticca Samuppada*), a core Buddhist doctrine.
iii. *Khandha-varga* (Aggregate Chapter) – Discusses the five aggregates (form, feeling, perception, volitional formations, consciousness) that constitute the self.
iv. *Salayatana-varga* (Six Sense Bases) – Explores the six sense faculties and their objects.
v. *Maha-varga* (Great Chapter) – Contains a variety of *suttas*, including some longer and more doctrinally significant teaching.

Each varga is subdivided into Samyutta, which each include a set of *sutras* on connected subjects.

d. *Anguttara Nikaya Suttas*

'*Anga*' means 'factor' and '*Uttara*' means 'further'. Therefore, Anguttara means some other *suttas*. They are divided into eleven *nipatas* (books). The nikaya consists of several thousand discourses ascribed to the Buddha and his chief disciples. They are arranged in eleven books.

Anguttara nikaya compiled the discourses contained in the Digha nikaya (the long discourse) and majjhima nikaya (the medium discourse), the aggregation of 186 dialogues of Gautama Buddha in order and systematically so that one might find almost all the psychology and ethics of Buddhism.

e. *Khuddaka Nikaya Suttas* (Division of Short Books)

It consists of fifteen books (eighteen in the Burmese edition). The Khuddaka Nikaya is the fifth and final *Nikaya* of the *Sutta Pitaka* in the Pali Canon of Theravada Buddhism. Despite its name – *Khuddaka* meaning 'small' or 'minor' – it contains some of the most important and well-known Buddhist texts. It is a diverse anthology, often considered a treasury of Buddhist literature.

i. *Khuddakapatha* – Short discourses and chants (e.g. Ten Precepts, Three Refuges).
ii. *Dhammapada* – The Path of Dhamma. A beloved anthology of 423 verses of the Buddha on ethics and wisdom.
iii. *Udana* – Inspired utterances of the Buddha, often poetic.

iv. *Itivuttaka* – The thus-saids – a mix of prose and verse on various teachings.
v. *Sutta Nipata* – The *Sutta* Collection. Early and profound discourses, including social and meditative themes.
vi. *Vimanavatthu* – Stories of the Celestial Mansions – rewards of meritorious deeds.
vii. *Petavatthu* – Tales of Spirits and Hungry Ghosts – suffering in the afterlife due to bad *karma*.
viii. *Theragatha* – Verses of the Elder Monks – expressing their spiritual experiences.
ix. *Therigatha* – Verses of the Elder Nuns – among the earliest records of women's religious poetry.
x. *Jataka* – Birth Stories of the Buddha's Past Lives – rich in moral and folk tradition.
xi. *Niddesa* – Commentarial exposition of parts of the *Sutta Nipata*.
xii. *Patisambhidamagga* – Analytical teachings on insight and knowledge.
xiii. *Apadana* – Spiritual biographies of monks and nuns.
xiv. *Buddhavamsa* – History of the Buddhas who preceded Gautama Buddha.
xv. *Cariyapitaka* – Stories of the Buddha's Past Lives – illustrating the Ten Perfections (*paramis*).

3. Abhidham Pitaka

Abhi means 'higher' and dhamma here refers to the teaching of the Buddha. Thus, *Abhidhamma* or *Abhidharma* constitutes the 'Higher Teaching' of the Buddha. It is the third and last of the Pitakas (baskets of discourses). It is the canonical collection of scripture of Theravada Buddhism.

The Buddha, it was believed, thought of the Abhidharma immediately after his enlightenment. Later, he repeated it to Sariputta who then transmitted it to his disciples. Modern Western scholars, however, opine that the origin of the Abhidharma Pitaka may be around 100 to 200 years after the death of the Buddha, i. e. , around the third century. Therefore, the seven Abhidharma works are generally claimed by scholars not to represent the words of the Buddha himself. They were written by disciples and scholars and thus developed independent doctrines.

Abhidharma, earlier, was considered as Metaphysics. It systematizes the Buddha's teachings into a precise, analytical framework. It breaks down reality into ultimate components (called *dhammas*). It examines the nature of mind and matter, mental states, and causality and offers tools for deep meditative insight and ethical refinement.

The Abhidharma Pitaka consists of seven books:

i. *Dhammasangani*
ii. *Vibhanga*
iii. *Dhatukatha* (*dhatukatha*)
iv. *Puggalapannatti*
v. *Kathavatthu*
vi. *Yamaka*
vii. *Patthana*

i. ***Dhammasangani:*** a 'Collection of Dharma' is a Buddhist scripture. It is the first of the seven texts of the Abhidharma Pitaka. The book begins with a condensed content in Pali which is a list of classifications of dhammas. Following the matika, the main body of the book is in four parts –

The first part deals with states of mind, listing and defining factors present in them; the second deals with material phenomena, classifying them numerically, by ones, twos, etc. The third part applies the material in the first two to explain the classifications in the matika. The fourth classifies in a more detailed way.

ii. ***Vibhanga:*** a Buddhist canonical text with eighteen chapters, and each deals with a particular topic:

- *khandha* (aggregate)
- *ayatana* (sense bases)
- *dhatu* (elements)
- *sacca* (truth)
- *indriya* (faculties)
- *paticca samuppada* (dependent origination)
- *satipatthana* (mindfulness)
- *sammappadhana* (right exertion)
- *iddhipada* (base of power)
- *bojjhanga* (enlightenment factor)
- *marga* (path)
- *jhana* (absorption)
- *appammanna* (immeasurables)
- *sikkhapada* (training rules)
- *patisambhida* (analysis)
- *nana* (knowledge)
- *khuddhaka vatthu* (smaller subjects)
- *dhamma hadaya* (heart of the Dhamma)

A typical chapter is divided into three parts: i) *Sutta* method, often consisting of quotations from the *Sutta Pitaka*; ii) *Abhidhamma* method with various lists of synonym or questions; iii) *Prccha* or Question method which applies the matika of the Dhammasangani and uses a question-and-answer format for a structured doctrinal review.

iii. ***Dhatukatha:*** Dhatukatha means discussion of Elements that covers both the matika and various topics, mostly from the Vibhanga, relating them to the 5 aggregates, 12 bases and 18 elements.

iv. ***Puggalapannatti*** means 'Designation of Individuals'. In the method of exposition this book resembles the Anguttara Nikaya of the *Sutta Pinaka*. Instead of dealing with various Dhammas, it deals with various types of individuals. There are ten chapters in this book. The first chapter deals with single individuals, the second with pairs, and so on.

v. ***Kathavatthu*** gives an account of opinions in which we find the name of the authors and date. It was made into a book by Tissa, the son of Moggoli about the year 250 BCE, at the Court of Ashoka. The book raises controversy against the ancient books to negate that there is nothing Metaphysical in Buddhism and thus also discards the superstitious view about the person Buddha.

vi. ***Yamaka*** – called 'The Book of Pairs' due to its method of treatment. Throughout the book a question and its converse are found grouped together. This book is divided into ten chapters, namely, Roots, Aggregates, Bases, Elements, Truths, Conditioned Things, Latent Dispositions, Consciousness, Dharma, and Indriya or Controlling Faculties.

vii. ***Patthana*** or The Book of Causal Relations. The book deals with 24 conditions in relation to the matika with details and numbers of answers. It deals with many cause and effects theories to organize into a coherent science of Buddhist doctrine (6-12).

Thus, *Abhidhamma Pitaka* may be called the summary of the Buddha's teachings in the *Suttas*. It is a scholastic analysis to unveil the general Buddhist principles. It may be called a science of Buddhist doctrine. It may also be called Buddhist Psychology.

7

FUNDAMENTALS OF BUDDHISM

The Mahavagga is the first volume of the Theravadin Khandhakas book from the *Vinaya Pitaka* in Buddhism. It includes accounts of the Buddha's and his great disciples' awakenings. It also had rules for *uposatha* days meant for the cleansing of the defiled mind, and monastic ordination.

'Wheel of life' or 'Chain of Causation' was first formulated in the Mahavagga in the following lines:

'Then the Blessed One (at the end of these seven days) during the first watch of the night fixed his mind upon the Chain of Causation, in direct and in reverse order:

'From Ignorance springs the *sankharas* (7-1), from the *sankharas* spring Consciousness, from Consciousness springs Name-and-Form, from Name-and-Form springs the six Provinces (of the six senses), from the six Provinces spring Contact, from Contact springs Sensation, from Sensation springs Thirst (or Desire), from Thirst springs Attachment, from Attachment springs Existence, from Existence springs Birth, from Birth spring Old Age and Death, grief, lamentation, suffering, dejection, and despair. Such is the origin of this whole mass of suffering.

'Again, by the destruction of Ignorance, which consists in the complete absence of lust, the *samkharas* are destroyed, by the destruction of the *samkharas* Consciousness is destroyed, by the destruction of Consciousness Name-and-Form is destroyed, by the destruction of Name-and-Form the six Provinces are destroyed, by the destruction of the six Provinces Contact is destroyed, by the destruction of Contact Sensation is destroyed, by the destruction of Sensation Thirst is destroyed, by the destruction of Thirst Attachment is destroyed, by the destruction of Attachment Existence is destroyed, by the destruction of Existence Birth is destroyed, by the destruction of Birth Old Age and Death, grief, lamentation, suffering, dejection, and despair are destroyed. Such is the cessation of this whole mass of suffering (7-1).'

From the above quote it is clear that *sankharas* or formations are going on. There is no permanent thing; everything is changing. An individual is subject to decay and death. In a word, animate and inanimate objects or materials are not permanent. So, nothing is being, everything is only becoming.

An individual possesses material qualities as well as mental qualities. The more the lower strata, the more the material aspects and less the mental aspects and vice versa.

As everything including an Individual or God is not a permanent one, and becoming, Sankhara or constant formations are going on. There is always putting together and also disintegration. Therefore, there is no permanent putting together. One is constantly changing and becoming different until it decays.

This is true in the case of all organic substances and living organisms, including us.

Early Buddhists believe in animism that says active things like animals, trees, and rivers are 'people like us' because, like human beings, they possess certain kinds of souls. It is these shared souls that imbue animals, trees, and rivers with a sentience that enables them like humans to move, grow, and breathe. By contrast, static things like stones are 'not persons' because they only share one soul in common with humans and lack the kind of sentience that would enable them to move and show signs of animated life, consciousness, and motivation. Buddhists from such a belief of animism which has come to them from their remote ancestors, sometimes, fail to understand the great 'Law of Impermanence'. According to Buddhist philosophy, this is ignorance and the worst of all superstitions.

The human beings, in Buddhism, are subject to delusion, resulting in suffering, and removal of that delusion resulting in the end of *dukkha*, is a central theme.

Marks of existence are discussed in the canons of the early Buddhist schools.

In the Pali tradition of the Theravada school, the three marks are referred to,

i. all *sankharas* (conditioned things) are impermanent;
ii. all *sankharas* are unsatisfactory, imperfect, unstable;
iii. all dharmas (conditioned or unconditioned things) have no unchanging self or soul. Therefore, belief in *anatta* or the doctrine of 'non-self' that says that no unchanging, permanent self or essence can be found in any phenomenon is the basis of Buddhist doctrine.

The source of sorrow is individuality. An individual always tries to keep away from sorrows and sufferings in life. And this separates an individual from the rest of existence. As one separates from the rest of existence so also disease, decay and death begin to act upon it. Therefore, and individual is always a limited one and a prey to ignorance. And ignorance leads an individual to make errors and thereby to sorrow. Whenever one becomes an individual, the six senses begin to play and it gives rise to ideas of attachment. It is not possible for an individual to satisfy all its desires and cravings mount up, giving rise to sorrow or pain. It is true for all individuals when they remain separate or isolated.

Isolation brings a self-centred attitude. People think they are quite separated from the outside world and people around them. They also think that they have no relation with the things of the past as well as they will have no relation with the things of the future. Only their own self is important to them. This is delusion by which people are isolated from the external world. Ignorance lies at the root of such delusion.

As a result, people fail to see their transitory existence as bubbles in the current of time immemorial that has gone in the past and that will continue to act in future.

In Pre-sectarian Buddhism or the earliest Buddhism, there prevailed the ideas and practices of Gautama Buddha himself and it continued to exist until the first documented split in the *sangha*. Contrary to the claim of doctrinal stability, early Buddhism was a dynamic movement. It may have included or incorporated other *sramanic* schools of thought, as well as Vedic and Jain ideas and practices.

Pre-sectarian Buddhism was originally one of the *sramanic* movements. The time of the Buddha was a time of urbanzation in India, and saw the growth of the sramanas, wandering philosophers who had rejected the authority of Vedas and Brahminic priesthood, and were intent on escaping samsara through various means, which involved the study of ascetic practices, and ethical behaviour.

The sramanas gave rise to different religious and philosophical schools, among which pre-sectarian Buddhism itself, Yoga and similar schools of Hinduism, Jainism, Ajivika, Ajnana, and Carvaka were the most important. It also gave rise to popular concepts in all major Indian religions such as samsara is an endless cycle of birth and death and moksha is liberation from that cycle.

The ideas of samsara, *karma* and rebirth show a development of thought in Indian religions: from the idea of single existence, at the end of which one was judged and punished and rewarded for one's deeds, or *karma*; to multiple existences with reward or punishment in an endless series of existences; and then attempts to gain release from this endless series. This release was the central aim of the sramana movement.

The Buddha at first sought 'the deathless' by overcoming death by those who entered the 'doors to the Deathless', or 'the gates of the Undying'. According to Conze, the Buddha saw death as a sign that 'something has gone wrong with us'. The Buddha saw death as brought on by an evil force, Mara, the Killer, who tempts us away from our true immortal selves and diverts us from the path which could lead us back to freedom. Our cravings keep us tied to Mara's realm. By releasing our attachments, we move beyond his realm, and gain freedom from samsara, the beginningless movement of death and rebirth.

Karma is the *cetana* (intentional actions) which keep us tied to samsara. Two views on the liberation from samsara can be discerned in the *sramanic* movements. Originally *karma* meant 'physical and mental activity'. One solution was to refrain from any physical or mental activity. The other solution was to see the real self as not participating in these actions, and to disidentify with those actions. According to Bronkhorst, the Buddha rejected both approaches. Nevertheless, these approaches can also be found in the Buddhist tradition, such as the four formless *jhanas*, and disidentification from the constituents of the self. Some noble scholars, however, have questioned whether *karma* played in the theory of rebirth in the early Buddhism.

'The deathless' is concerned with the here and now. Only after this realisation did one become acquainted with the doctrine of rebirth. Bronkhorst disagrees, and concludes that the Buddha introduced a concept of *karma* that differed considerably from the commonly held views of his time. According to Bronkhorst, not physical and mental activities as such were seen as responsible for rebirth, but intentions and desire (7-2).

In this context, Rhys Davids says, 'There is a real identity between a man in his present life and in the future. But the identity is not in a conscious soul which shall fly out away from his body after he is dead. The real identity is that of cause and effect. A man thinks he began to be a few years twenty, forty, sixty years ago. There is some truth in that; but in a much larger, deeper and a truer sense he has been (in the causes of which he is the result) for countless ages in the past; and those some causes (of which is the temporary effect) will continue in other like temporary forms through countless ages to come. In that sense alone, according to Buddhism, each of us has after death a continuing life' (7-3).

Unlike the concept of the soul found in early animistic beliefs and in Christian theology, Rhys Davids says, 'The fact underlining all these theories is acknowledged to be a very real one. The history of an individual does not begin with his birth, but has been endless ages in the making; and he cannot sever himself from his surroundings, no, not for an hour. The tiniest snowdrop droops its fairy head just so much and no more, because it is balanced by the universe. It is a snowdrop, not an oak, and just that kind of snowdrop, because it is the outcome of the *karma* of an endless series of past existences, and because it did not begin to be when the flower opened, or when the mother plant first peeped above the ground, or first met the embraces of the sun, or when the bulb begin to shoot above the soil, or at any time which you and I can fix'.

Therefore, it is not so important for a Buddhist to seek salvation as to do good actions in his present life. These good actions will remain when he will be no more and help some others to advance. Still, he can reach salvation to some extent in his present world and therefore he shouldn't waste time for attaining the supposed happiness of heaven which is nothing but delusion. Escaping from such delusion that takes pride in individuality, a Buddhist may proceed to the path of a new and enlightened one. The Buddhist books deal with paths leading to escape from delusions and attaining the plane of nirvana.

The three fundamental ideas of Buddhism that present a view of life quite contradictory to the animistic notion accepted in the west is essential for us to understand.

These are Aniccam, *Dukkha* and *Anattam*, that is,

- The Impermanence of every Individual;
- The Sorrow inherent in individuality;
- The Non-reality of any abiding principle.

When the Buddha, after attaining nirvana, was received by the first five converts, he said what may be called the solution of the above three fundamental doctrines:

'The *Tathagata*,' the Buddha continued, 'does not seek celebration in austerities but neither does he for that reason indulge in worldly pleasures, nor live in abundance. The *Tathagata* has found the middle path. There are two extremes O *bhikkhus*, which the man who has given up the world ought not to follow – the habitual practice, on the one hand, of self-indulgence which is unworthy, vain and fit only for the worldly-minded; and the habitual practice, on the other hand, of self-mortification, which is painful, useless and unprofitable. Neither abstinence from fish or flesh, nor going naked, nor shaving the head, nor wearing matted hair, not dressing in a rough garment, nor covering oneself with dirt, nor sacrificing to Agni, will cleanse a man who is not free from delusions. Reading the Vedas, making offerings to priests, or sacrifices to the gods, self-mortification by heat or cold, and many such penances performed for the sake of immortality do not cleanse the man who is not free from delusions. Anger, drunkenness, obstinacy, bigotry, deception, envy, self-praise, disparaging others, superciliousness, and evil intentions constitute uncleanness; not verily the eating of flesh.

'A middle path *bhikkhus*, avoiding the two extremes, has been discovered by the *Tathagata* – a path which opens the eyes, and bestows understanding, which leads to peace of mind, to the higher wisdom, to full enlightenment, to nirvana!

'What is the middle path, O *bhikkhus*, avoiding these two extremes discovered by the *Tathagata* – that path which opens the eyes, and bestows understanding, which leads to peace of mind, to higher wisdom, to full enlightenment, to nirvana?

'Let me teach you, O *bhikkhus*, the middle path, which keeps value from both extremes. By suffering, the emaciated devotee produces confusion and sickly thoughts in his mind. Mortification is not conducive even to worldly knowledge; how much less to a triumph over the senses!

'He who fills his lamp with water will not dispel the darkness, and he who tries to light a fire with rotten wood will fail. And how can anyone be free from self by leading a wretched life, if he does not succeed in quenching the fires of lust, if he still hankers after either worldly or heavenly pleasures? But he in whom self has become extinct is free from lust; he will desire neither worldly nor evenly pleasures, and the satisfaction of his natural wants will not defile him. However, let him be moderate, let him eat and drink according to the needs of the body.

'Sensuality is enervating; the self-indulgent man is a slave to his passions, and pleasure-seeking is dangerous and vulgar.

'But to satisfy the necessity of life is not evil, to keep the body in good health is a duty; for otherwise we shall not be able to trim the lamp of wisdom, and keep our mind strong and clear. Water surrounds the lotus flower, but does not wait its petals.

'This is the middle path, O *bhikkhus*, that keeps aloof from both extremes.'

Now the blessed one set the wheel of the most excellent law rolling, and began to preach to the five *bhikkhus*, opening to them the gate of immortality, and showing them the bliss of nirvana.

The Buddha said:

'The spokes of the wheel are the rules of pure conduct; justice is the uniformity of their length; wisdom is the tyre; modesty and thoughtfulness are the hub in which the immovable axle of truth is fixed.

'He who recognizes the existence of suffering, its cause, its remedy, and its cessation has fathomed the four noble truths. He will walk in the right path.

'Right views will be the torch to light his way. Right aspirations will be his guide. Right speech will be his dwelling place on the road. His gait will be straight, for it is right behaviour. His replacements will be the right way of earning his livelihood. Right efforts will be his steps; right thought his breath; and right contemplation will give him the peace that follows in his footprints.

'Now this, O *bhikkhus*, is the Noble Truth concerning suffering?

'Birth is attended with pain; decay is painful, disease is painful, death is painful. Union with the unpleasant is painful, painful is separation from the pleasant; and any craving that is unsatisfied, that too is painful.

'This, then O *bhikkhus*, is the Noble Truth concerning the suffering.

"Now this O *bhikkhus*, is the Noble Truth concerning the origin of suffering?

'Verily, it is that craving which causes the renewal of existence, accompanied by sensual delight, seeking satisfaction, now here, now there, the craving for the gratification of the passions, the craving for a future life, and the craving for happiness in this life.

'This, then, O *bhikkhus*, is the Noble Truth concerning the origin of suffering?

'Now, this, O *bhikkhus*, is the Noble Truth concerning the destruction of suffering?

'Verily, it is the destruction in which no passion remains of this very thirst; it is the laying aside of the being free from, the dwelling no longer upon this thirst.

'Now, this, O *bhikkhus*, is the noble truth concerning the way which leads to the destruction of sorrow? Verily! It is the Noble Eightfold Path; that is to say:

i. Right views;
ii. Right Aspirations;
iii. Right Speech;
iv. Right Behaviour;
v. Right Livelihood;
vi. Right Effort;
vii. Right Thoughts; and
viii. Right Contemplation.

'Now, then, O *bhikkhus*, is the Noble Truth concerning the destruction of sorrow?

'By the practice of loving kindness, I have attained liberation of heart, and thus I am assured that I shall never return in renewed births. I have even now attained nirvana (7-4).'

Now, in order to move through the Noble Path, one is to break the ten '*Samyojanas*' or Fetters.

The Pali canon's *Sutta Pitaka* identifies ten 'fetters of becoming'.

i. *Sakkaya-ditthi* or belief in a self. By believing in 'self' one suffers permanently from self-delusion. It, thus, isolates a person from others. Every Buddhist has to break this form of delusion first in order to start on the way to Buddhism. People having self-deception fail to find their true identity and do not think that they are transient in this world. Therefore, they fail to give up the delusion of self, and thereby do not destroy their sorrows nor enter the path of Buddhism.

ii. *Vicikiccha* or doubt which every Buddhist has to break. *Vicikiccha* is being of two minds about the meaning of the Four Noble Truths. One is doubtful about the Four Noble Truths. Every Buddhist has to clear the doubt themselves and then they can strive for their own salvation.

iii. *Silabbata-paramasa* or attachment to rites and rituals is the third through which one has to do away with false beliefs now. No obsession with the strict observance of rules, rites, and rituals will lead to salvation as seen in the sramanas. The cultivation of insight and understanding while following those rules, rites and rituals should be observed.

iv. *Kamacchando* or sensual desire to gratify the sense by indulging in five sense organs. Sensual desire is thus aroused and it causes distraction from meditation.

v. *Vyapado* or ill will is harmful intention to injure others. The ill will mars the very intention of love for meditation. As Buddha says, 'In order to break it, one should submit to love and sympathy and thus weaken the strength of this fifth fetter until it is destroyed' (The Buddhist Dictionary).

vi. *Ruparago* or lust for material existence is an illusion for material things and material life.
vii. *Aruparago* or lust for immaterial existence is lust for rebirth in a formless realm. It is a desire for future life in heaven.
viii. *Mano* (conceit).
ix. *Uddhacca* or restlessness.
x. *Avijja* or ignorance.

The first five fetters are referred to as 'lower fetters' and are eradicated upon becoming a non-returner; and, the last five fetters are referred to as 'higher fetters' eradicated by an *arahant*.

The *Dhammasangani* in the *Abhidhamma Pitaka* provides an alternate list of ten fetters which is also found in the Khuddaka Nikaya's Culla Niddesa and in post-canonical commentaries. They are:

i. *kamaraga* (attachment to sensuality);
ii. *patigha* (anger);
iii. *mana* (conceit);
iv. *ditthi* (views);
v. *vicikiccha* (doubt);
vi. *silabbata-paramasa* (attachment to rites and rituals);
vii. *bhavaraga* (attachment to existence);
viii. *issa* (jealousy);
ix. *macchariya* (stinginess, greed);
x. *avijja* (ignorance).

FOUR STAGES OF AWAKENING

In Early Buddhism and Theravada there are four stages of awakening that culminate in full awakening (Bodhi) as an *Arahant* (Arahat).

These four stages are –

a. *Sotapanna* (stream-enterer),
b. *Sakadagami* (once-returner),
c. *Anagami* (non-returner), and
d. *Arahant*.

The oldest Buddhist texts define people as noble (*ariya-puggala*) who are at one of these four stages and the community of such persons as the noble *sangha* or *ariya-sangha*.

In the *Sutta Pitaka* several types of Buddhist practitioners are described, according to their level of attainment. The standard is four, but there are also longer descriptions with more types. The four are the Stream-enterer, Once-returner, Non-returner and the *Arahant*.

In the *Visuddhimagga* the five stages are the culmination of the seven purifications. The descriptions are elaborated and harmonised, giving the same sequence of purifications before attaining each of the four paths and fruits.

The Visuddhimagga stresses the importance of *Prajna* (panna), insight into *anatta* (anatman) and the Buddhist teachings, as the main means to liberation. *Vipassana* has a central role in this.

A 'Stream-enterer' (*Sotapanna*) is free from:

1. Identity view, the belief that there is an unchanging self or soul in the five impermanent *skandhas*;
2. Attachment to rites and rituals;
3. Doubt about the teachings;
   A "Once-returner" has greatly attenuated;
4. Sensual desire;

5. Ill will;

   A 'non-returner' is free from sensual desire and ill will

   An *Arahant* is free from all of the five lower fetters and the five higher fetters, which are:

6. Attachment to the four meditative absorptions, which have form;
7. Attachment to the four formless absorptions;
8. Conceit;
9. Restlessness;
10. Ignorance.

The four stages that culminates in Arhantship may be dealt with for the clear understanding:

A. ***Sotapanna*** (stream-entrant or stream-enterer):
Sotapanna or stream-entrant or stream-enterer is a person who has seen the dharma and thereby has dropped the first three fetters (*samyojana*). A man who was attached to self-view (*sakkaya-ditthi*), clinging to rites and rituals (*Silabbata-paramasa*), and sceptical indecision (*Vicikitsa*) now enters a stream which leads to a vast ocean, nirvana.

The first moment of the attainment, overcoming the first three fetters. is termed the path of stream-entry (*Sotapatti-magga*). The person who experiences it is called a stream-winner (*Sotapanna*). He is believed to attain an intuitive grasp of the dharma and has unshakable confidence in the Buddha, dharma, and *sangha*. The *Sotapanna* is said to have 'opened the eye of the Dhamma' (*dhamma cakkhu*), because they have realised that whatever arises will cease (impermanence). The *Sotapanna* may state this about himself: 'Hell is ended; animal wombs are ended; the state of the hungry shades is ended; states of deprivation, destitution, the bad bourns are ended! I am a stream-winner, steadfast, never again destined for states of woe, headed for self-awakening' (7-5).

The early Buddhist texts say that a stream-entrant will no longer be born in the animal womb, or Hell realms, nor as a hungry ghost. The pathways to unfortunate rebirth destinations (*duggati*) have been closed to them (7-6). A *Sotapanna* will have to be reborn at most only seven more times in the human or heavenly worlds before attaining nirvana (5-7). But it is not necessary for a *Sotapanna* to be reborn seven more times before attaining nirvana, as an ardent practitioner may progress to the higher stages in the same life by making an aspiration and persistent effort to reach the final goal of nirvana.

According to Buddha, there are three types of *Sotapanna* – *satta khatu-parama* (one with seven births at the utmost), *kolankola* (one passing from one noble family to another two to three times), and *eka-biji* (germinating only once more).

Again, a *Sotapanna* will not commit six wrong actions:

1. Murdering one's own mother.
2. Murdering one's own father.
3. Murdering an *arahant*.
4. Maliciously injuring the Buddha to the point of drawing blood.
5. Deliberately creating a schism in the monastic community.
6. Taking another teacher (besides Buddha).

B. ***Sakadagami*** or returning once or once-returner, is a partially enlightened person, who has cut off the first three chains with which the ordinary mind is bound, and significantly weakened the fourth and fifth. *Sakadagami*ship is the second stage of the four stages of enlightenment. He will be reborn into the realm of the senses at most once more. If, however, they attain the next stage of enlightenment (Anagamiship) in this life, they will not come back to this world. A *Sakadagami* is free from the three specific chains or fetters Besides, he also significantly weakened the chains of *Kama-raga* (Sensuous craving) and *Bayapada* (Ill will).

Thus, the *Sakadagami* is an intermediate stage between the *Sotapanna*, who still has comparatively strong sensuous desire and ill-will, and the Anagami, who is completely free from sensuous desire and ill-will. His mind is very pure. Thoughts connected with greed, hatred and delusion do not arise often, and when they do, do not become obsessive.

C. *Anagamin*

An *Anagamin* (non-returning) is a partially enlightened person who has cut off the first five fetters and is not reborn into the human world after death. He has his place into the heaven of the Pure Abode where he attains full enlightenment or Arhantship.

D. **Arhant or Arhat**

In Buddhism, an Arhant or Arhat is one who has gained insight into the true nature of existence and has achieved nirvana. He is liberated from the endless cycle of rebirth.

The understanding of the concept has changed over the centuries, and varies between different schools of Buddhism and different regions. Mahayana Buddhist teachings urge followers to take up the path of a bodhisattva, and to not fall back to the level of arhats and sravakas.

In pre-Buddhist India, the term arhat was closely associated with miraculous power and asceticism. Buddhists made a sharp distinction between their arhats and Indian holy men, and miraculous powers were no longer central to arhat identity or mission.

In Theravada Buddhism, an arhat is a person who has eliminated all the unwholesome roots which underlie the fetters. They upon their death will not be reborn in any world, since the bonds (fetters) that bind a person to samsara have been finally dissolved. In the Pali Canon, the word *Tathagata* is sometimes used as a synonym for arhat, though the former usually refers to the Buddha alone.

After attainment of nirvana, the five aggregates (physical forms, sensations, perception, mental formations and consciousness) will continue to function, sustained by physical bodily vitality. This attainment is termed the nirvana element with a residue remaining. But once the arhat passes away and with the disintegration of the physical body, the five aggregates will cease to function, hence ending all traces of existence in the phenomenal world and thus total release from the misery of samsara. It would then be termed the nirvana element without residue remaining. *Parinirvana* occurs at the death of an arhat.

In Theravada Buddhism, the Buddha himself is first identified as an arhat, as are his enlightened followers, because they are free from all defilements, existing without greed, hatred, delusion, ignorance and craving.

In the Pali canon, Ananda states that he knows monastics to achieve nirvana in one of four ways:

i. one develops insight preceded by serenity;

ii. one develops serenity preceded by insight;
iii. one develops serenity and insight in a stepwise fashion;
iv. one's mind becomes seized by excitation about the dhamma and, as a consequence, develops serenity and abandons the fetters.

For those that have destroyed greed and hatred with some residue of delusion, are called Anagami (non-returner). Anagamis will not be reborn into the human world after death, but into the heaven of the Pure Abodes, where only Anagamis live. There, they will attain full enlightenment.

There is a difference seen in the Mahayana doctrine. In Mahayana Buddhism, it is said that nirvana must be sought without being sought, and practice must be done without being practiced.

A range of views on the attainment of arhats existed in the early Buddhist schools but most of them regarded arhats as being imperfect in their attainments compared to buddhas.

8

MAHAYANA IN BRIEF

Mahayana that literally means 'Great Vehicle' is one of the important branches of Buddhism. The branch developed in India in the first century BCE. Mahayana had its own *Sutras*, beside accepting the main scriptures and *sutras* of early Buddhism. *Vajrayana* (*Vajrajana* in Sanskrit) originates from it. Mahayana shows the bodhisattva path to enable one to be 'fully awakened' and so it is also called the 'Bodhisattva Vehicle' (BodhisattvaYana). BodhisattvaYana or the vehicle of a bodhisattva seeks Buddhahood for the benefit of all sentient beings. The production of Mahayana *sutras* spans a period of some six or seven centuries.

References to Mahayana are found in Lotus *Sutra* or *Saddharma Pundarika Sutra* which originated between the first century BCE and the first century CE. It had its trace in an earlier Gandhari Prakrit version in the term *mahajana* meaning 'great knowing'. Later the term Mahayana in Prakrit may have come to be converted to Mahayana in Sanskrit.

In Chinese, Emperor Ling of Han translated the Lotus *Sutra* in which the term appeared. It was also used in some other texts and Agamas there, though Chinese scholars differ regarding the interpretation of the term.

There are numerous theories about its origin. Jean Przyluski gave 'The lay origins theory' which says that the laypersons first developed Mahayana which was like the text '*Vimalakirti Sutra*'.

Next comes the 'Mahasamghika origin theory' which says that Mahayana developed within the Mahasamghika tradition. Scholars like Hendrik Kern, A. K. Warder and Paul Williams defend it saying that elements of Mahayana had traces in Mahasamghika communities found in the area along the Krishna River in the Andhra region of southern India from the first century BCE and afterwards.

Scholars like Paul Harrison and Paul Williams contradict the Mahasamghika origin theory saying that Mahayana did not develop as the separate school but certain set of ideals developed and they might have developed the bodhisattvas concept.

Another theory called the 'forest hypothesis' says thatMahayana was developed by *aranyavasam* or forest dwelling ascetics. Scholars like Paul Harrison, Jan Nattier and Reginald Ray defended this.

Again, 'The cult of the book theory' says that a group of monks memorised the *sutras* kept in shrines and Mahayana *sutras* originated from them. Scholar like Gregory Schopen states that.

According to David Drewes, Mahayana was primarily a textual movement, focused on the revelation, preaching, and dissemination of Mahayana *sutras* that developed within, and never really departed from traditional Buddhist social and institutional structures.

Mahayana was a minority movement in India but it was an intellectually vibrant movement. It came to develop as various schools of thought. In fact, it was the Golden Age of Indian

Buddhist Philosophy that began from the beginning of the first millennium CE up to the 7th century.

Some important Mahayana traditions are Prajnaparamita, Madhyamaka, Yogacara, Buddha-nature or Tathagatagarbha, and the school of Dignaga and Dharmakirti as the last and most recent. Major early figures include Nagarjuna, Aryadeva, Asvaghosa, Asanga, Vasubandhu, and Dignaga. Mahayana Buddhists seem to have been active in the Kushan Empire (30–375 CE), a period that saw great missionary and literary activities by Buddhists. This is supported by the works of the historian Taranatha.

Some kind of popular support for Mahayana was traced in Mathura. It was in the 4th and 5th century CE but very few manuscripts have been found before the fifth century.

It was after the fifth century when the movement began to develop. The three Chinese pilgrims, such as Fa-hien (337–422 CE), Huen Tsang (602–664), I-tsing (635–713 CE) during their travel to India, saw monasteries and described them in their writings. They wrote of Mahayana as well as other monasteries where monks of both the sects lived together. After that, Mahayana Buddhism and its institutions began to grow with debate and discussions, the culmination of which was Nalanda, a monastic university complex in the 5th-century CE during Gupta emperor, Kumaragupta I. Then established Vikramashila later in 783 CE to 820 CE under Dharmapala. Both were the centres of Mahayana Buddhism.

Three writers should be singled out in this connection. The first is Nagarjuna, a monk probably from the south of India who lived in the second century CE and was the author of the *Madhyamaka-karika* ('Verses on the Middle') as well as a number of other works. He is revered by the Buddhists of China and Tibet as the founding father of one of the principal 'Sastra' systems of

Mahayana philosophy, namely the *Madhyamaka* or *Sunyavada*.

The other two authors can be taken together. Indeed, tradition has it that they were brothers. They are Asatiga and Vasubandhu, who lived in north India at the end of the fourth or beginning of the fifth century CE. Together these two are regarded as the founding fathers of the other great 'Sastra' school of the Mahayana, namely which expounded the theory that apart from *cittavijiitina* (consciousness or mind) and the *vijiiapti* (ideas and information) it processes, there is nothing.

Mahayana Buddhism as a more or less separate tradition of Buddhism, with its clearly defined subdivisions and philosophical schools, is to some extent the outcome of the history of Chinese and Tibetan Buddhism. As it evolved in China and Tibet, Buddhism came to adopt an exclusively Mahayanist outlook in a way that it never did in India. As Buddhism began to fade from the Indian scene in the eleventh and twelfth centuries, the Buddhists of China, Japan, and Korea to the east, and Tibet and Mongolia to the north, were left as heirs to the Indian Mahayanist vision. To the south the Buddhists of Sri Lanka and south-east Asia became the only surviving representatives of the perspective of the non-Mahayana. Yet we must remember that much of what modern Buddhists in Sri Lanka, China, or Tibet have inherited from the past was held in common by both the Mahayana and non-Mahayana tradition (8-1).

In short, Mahayana includes the classic Buddhist doctrines, the Nikaya and Agamas in early Buddhism that again include the Middle Way, Dependent origination, the Four Noble Truths, the Noble Eightfold Path, the Three Jewels, the Three marks of existence and the *bodhipaksa dharma* (aids to awakening). Along with this it further accepts some of the ideas found in

Buddhist Abhidharma thought. With all these, Mahayana has its own texts and doctrines. In fact, the main motive behind Mahayana is to motivate in achieving Buddhahood for the sake and welfare of other beings. Accordingly, Mahayana is not to be bound to a particular institutional identity. It relies heavily on inner motivation and vision which can lead to attaining full Buddhahood and therefore, it has no specific school or sect.

The central elements of Mahayana are Buddhas and bodhisattvas. There are various Buddhas and powerful bodhisattvas forming buddha kshetra. The Buddhas are *Amitabha* (Infinite Light), *Aksobhya* (the Imperturbable), *Bhaisajya guru* (Medicine guru) and *Vairocana* (the Illuminator). The Buddhas are transcendental and immeasurable and in one life-span of the Buddha (Gautam Buddha) who achieved Buddhahood through countless of Kalpas ago. Now, he is actively devising ways to teach and help all sentient beings as a spiritual king. Thus, Gautam Buddha's life and death on earth is but a mere appearance.

Various Mahayana texts present two models for the nature of the bodhisattvas. One is the idea that a bodhisattva must postpone their awakening until full Buddhahood is attained. After reaching Buddhahood, he passes on to nirvana and does not return. The second model says that there are two kinds of nirvana. One is through arhat and the other, *apratistha* that allows a Buddha to remain forever engaged in the world.

The Mahayanists think that the Mahayana bodhisattva path is a superior spiritual path over the paths of those who seek Arhantship or solitary Buddhahood for their own sake. On the other hand, they resolve to liberate all other sentient beings from samsara by becoming a Buddha.

The term bodhisattva is applicable to any person from the moment they intend to become a Buddha. The bodhisattva path is said to take three or four *asamkheyyas* (incalculable eons or Kalpas). It requires a huge number of lifetimes of practice to complete. The bodhisattva's spiritual path is bodhicitta pada which is a system of arising of the Awakening Mind to become a Buddha and work for the welfare of all beings. The Indian Acharya Shantideva taught meditation in his *Bodhicaryavatara* to achieve the bodhisattva. Other Indian masters like Atisha and Kamalashila also taught meditation in which one contemplates how all beings have been our close relatives or friends in past lives (8-2).

Theravada and other early Buddhist schools held that becoming a bodhisattva required a prediction of one's future Buddhahood in the presence of a living Buddha. Some Mahayana *sutras* like the Lotus *Sutra* look upon the bodhisattva path as being universal and open to everyone. The bodhisattva path is intended for the practice of a set of virtues called paramitas like giving, ethical discipline, patient endurance, diligence, meditation and transcendent wisdom.

There are various Mahayana Buddhist texts intended for bodhisattva practice.

The Dasa Bhumika Sutra as well as other texts also outline a series of bodhisattva levels or spiritual stages (Bhumis) on the path to Buddhahood though there is disagreement on the number of stages.

The idea of Upaya or expedient techniques refers to any effective method or technique that leads beings to awakening and nirvana. This doctrine states that the Buddha adapts his teaching to whomever he is teaching, out of compassion.

Ekayana means 'One Vehicle'. The Buddha described three different paths: for disciples, for solitary Buddhas, and for bodhisattvas. But all of them lead to the same destination – becoming a Buddha. So in the end, there is only one true path.

The Yogacara School famously defended an alternative theory that held that not all beings could become Buddhas.

Prajnaparamita is a deep knowledge of reality which Buddhas and bodhisattvas attain. It is also associated with the *sunyata* or emptiness of dharmas and their illusory nature (Maya). This emptiness says that all phenomena are also described as *Anupada* or unarisen and *ajata* or unborn. *Prajnaparamita Sutra* explains 'not grasping at form, not grasping at sensation, perception, volitions and cognition, including not grasping or taking up even correct Buddhist ideas or mental signs such as "not-self", "emptiness", bodhicitta, vows'.

MADHYAMAKA

Madhyamaka or Middle theory or Centrism is also known as sunyada or the emptiness theory. It was founded by the Nagarjuna of the second century. This philosophical tradition says that anything that has an independent existence cannot be dependently originated. Madhyamaka claims that while one can speak of things existing in a conventional, relative sense, they do not exist inherently in an ultimate sense. It also argues that emptiness itself is also 'empty', it does not have an absolute inherent existence of its own. Since everything is empty of true existence, all things are just conceptualizations including the theory of emptiness. Therefore, all concepts must ultimately be abandoned in order to truly understand the nature of things.

Vijnanavada is the doctrine of consciousness which later became the central theory of a major philosophical movement – 'Yogacara' during the Gupta period. This school of thought is associated with the *Samdhinirmocana Sutra*. This *Sutra* says that sunyavada is not the final teaching of the Buddha. But the *Paramartha-satya* or ultimate truth is that all dharmas are only *citta*, (consciousness) *vijnana* or *vijnapti* perceptions (and that seemingly "external" objects (or "internal" subjects) do not really exist apart from the dependently originated flow of mental experience.

Buddha-nature is another concept that says that all sentient beings already have a pure Buddha-essence within themselves. Buddha-nature has a wide range of meanings in Indian Buddhism and later in East Asian and Tibetan Buddhist literature. Broadly speaking it refers to the belief that the luminous mind or the natural and true state of the mind is pure and inherently present in every sentient being. It is eternal and unchanging.

In conclusion, we can say that there is no unity in the Mahayana religion. It is characterised by a great degree of diversity and the amazing amount of tolerance. There is more than one Buddha. There are a number of Buddhas endowed with the highest intelligence and love. They too are working constantly to save the world. There have been an infinite number of these Buddhas in the past, and there will be an infinite number in the future. All of these Buddhas are transitory manifestations of the one eternal being (8-3).

The Chief Characteristics and Doctrines of Mahayana Buddhism – King, Martin Luther, Jr. Stanford, The Martin Luther King, Jr. Research and Education Institute).

9

IMPACT OF BUDDHISM IN PRESENT TIMES

> 'Peace comes from within. Do not seek it without.'
>
> – The Buddha

In a world overwhelmed by external noise and internal unrest, the teachings of Buddhism offer a quiet refuge – a path to clarity, compassion, and meaningful living. Rooted in ancient India over 2,500 years ago, Buddhism is more than a religion; it is a profound way of life. Today, as humanity faces unprecedented challenges – technological overload, environmental crisis, mental health epidemics, social division, and spiritual emptiness – the timeless principles of Buddhism provide wisdom that is urgently relevant. Gautam Buddha is a valuable component of India's cultural history. One of the main features is that he did not unnecessarily contradict the Brahmanical tradition nor asked to give up the Sacred Fire with which so many ancient traditions and so many religious emotions were effective.

1. Mindfulness

Buddhism has impacted the world in many ways. At the very heart of Buddhist practice lies **mindfulness,** the gentle art of paying full attention to the present moment. In our times, where endless notifications, rapid news cycles, and relentless multitasking dominate daily life, mindfulness stands as a quiet revolution. It calls us back – to our breath, to our body, to the reality unfolding in front of us. Rather than escaping the chaos, mindfulness trains us to face it with equanimity. It teaches the mind to observe without judgment, to witness thoughts and emotions as passing phenomena, not absolute truths. In doing so, it transforms reaction into wise response and chaos into clarity.

Modern science affirms what Buddhist practitioners have known for centuries. Programmes like Mindfulness-Based Stress Reduction (MBSR) and Mindfulness-Based Cognitive Therapy (MBCT) – rooted in Buddhist meditation techniques – have become mainstream tools in the treatment of anxiety, depression, trauma, and chronic pain. Research from institutions like Harvard and Oxford has shown that regular mindfulness practice rewires the brain, enhancing areas linked to attention, empathy, and emotional regulation.

But mindfulness is more than a clinical intervention. It is a way of being – a return to the wholeness of life. It helps us eat with awareness, listen deeply, work with intention, and rest fully. In a world thirsty for presence and overwhelmed by distraction, mindfulness offers not an escape, but a homecoming – a steady light in the flickering storm.

> 'When we are mindful, deeply in touch with the present moment, our understanding of what is going on deepens, and we begin to be filled with acceptance, joy, peace and love.'
>
> – Thich Nhat Hanh

2. Compassion: Healing a Fractured World

Buddhism emphasizes *karuna* **(compassion)** and *metta* (loving-kindness) as essential virtues. In an increasingly polarised world, where communities are torn apart by hatred, inequality, and conflict, these teachings offer a path to healing. Compassion encourages us to see others not as opponents, but as fellow beings who, like us, seek happiness and wish to avoid suffering.

Programmes promoting social-emotional learning (SEL) in schools and empathy-based leadership in workplaces draw heavily from this Buddhist principle.

> "Hatred does not cease by hatred, but only by love; this is the eternal rule."
>
> – Dhammapada, Verse 5

3. Non-Violence and Peaceful Coexistence

The Buddhist path is rooted in ahimsa (non-violence) – not merely the absence of physical violence, but an active attitude of peace and gentleness. In modern times, where warfare, domestic violence, and online abuse are rampant, ahimsa teaches restraint, understanding, and respectful dialogue.

Great leaders like Mahatma Gandhi and Martin Luther King Jr. drew inspiration from Buddhist and Jain ideas of non-violence to lead civil rights movements with dignity and moral strength.

4. Simplicity and Sustainability in a Consumerist Culture

Modern life promotes consumption as the path to happiness. Buddhism, however, teaches the virtue of simplicity, detachment, and *santutthi* (contentment). The Middle Way taught by the Buddha encourages balance – not extreme austerity, nor indulgent luxury.

In a world reeling from ecological crises – climate change, deforestation, pollution – this call for moderation is vital. Living simply and mindfully reduces waste and fosters a harmonious relationship with the earth.

> 'Just as a candle cannot burn without fire, men cannot live without a spiritual life.'
>
> – The Buddha

5. The Path to Inner Freedom

While the world chases outer success – status, money, possessions – Buddhism points us inward. The Four Noble Truths and the Eightfold Path provide a framework for understanding the root of suffering (*dukkha*) and how to transcend it. This inner journey leads to nirvana, a state of profound peace beyond craving and ego. Even for non-practitioners, the message is clear: true happiness is not found outside, but in mastering the mind.

6. Equality and Interconnectedness

Buddhism rejects discrimination of race, class, or caste. All beings are seen as interconnected and equally worthy of respect. The concept of pratityasamutpada (interdependence) affirms that our actions ripple across time, space, and lives.

This view aligns with modern calls for inclusivity, diversity, and social justice. The Buddhist monastic order was one of the first spiritual institutions to accept people regardless of caste or status.

7. Relevance to Mental Health

The teachings of Buddhism offer powerful tools for mental well-being. Concepts like anicca (impermanence), *dukkha* (suffering), and *anattā* (non-self) help individuals come to terms with change, loss, and identity crises. Meditation calms the mind, reduces anxiety, and builds emotional resilience.

Therapists and psychiatrists across the globe are now integrating Buddhist psychology into modern therapy. Mindful breathing, self-awareness, and loving-kindness meditations are routinely prescribed to help with depression and emotional regulation.

In essence, Buddhist principles are not merely spiritual ideals – they are deeply practical tools for creating a more peaceful, compassionate, and conscious society. They help us cultivate patience in conflict, calm in chaos, and love in the face of fear.

As the modern world searches for meaning amid material success, the gentle wisdom of the Buddha continues to shine as a timeless torch, illuminating the path to inner peace and collective well-being.

The Buddhist faith, due to its emphasis on peaceful co-existence and its wide pan-Asian presence is given preference as the soft power foreign policy of India by the government under Narendra Modi, the prime minister of the country. Similarly, the Government has taken an initiative to incorporate

Buddhist heritage in order to form a basis for further diplomatic, economic, cultural, and strategic associations within its foreign policy. The already existing transnational network for Buddhism that has played an important role in the lives of millions across the world is decided to be used with much vigour for Indian foreign policy. The pan-Asian presence of the religion and its importance for national identities in the region, coupled with its image as a peaceful religion makes it ideal for soft power diplomacy, with its focus on non-coercive power (9-4).

In fact, India has more advantage than other pan- Asian nations to use Buddhism as soft power foreign-policy as being the pioneer of the faith. India can not only claim its legitimacy but also boast of Buddhist sites and places, indispensable for the cultivation of the faith. Buddhist sites like Bodh Gaya, Sarnath, and Nalanda, Vaishali, Kushinagar are not only sites but also the places where Buddhist philosophy had once been cultivated. Again, from Theravada Buddhism came the Tibetan Buddhism and so, India has naturally an additional advantage as the originator of Theravada Buddhism. India also has the support for the Dalai Lama and the Tibetan religious system in the city of Dharamshala in the face of Chinese opposition.

Thus, Buddhism and state diplomacy which dates back from the reign of Ashoke is India's potential force to build up an unparalleled soft power diplomacy to conquer the neighbouring nations. This ancient geopolitical tool is to be made for use to meet the challenges of the new millennium and India rightly undertakes it.

THE WIDER IMPACT OF BUDDHISM IN THE MODERN WORLD

Beyond its principles and teachings, Buddhism's influence can be seen in multiple domains of contemporary life – from personal development to global peacebuilding, from medical science to interfaith harmony. Its soft but steady impact continues to shape thought, behavior, and global dialogue.

1. Personal Transformation and Self-Realization

Buddhism begins with the individual. Its transformative power lies in helping people understand the nature of suffering and awaken to their full potential. Through meditation, ethical conduct, and self-inquiry, countless people across the world have found clarity, calmness, and renewed purpose.

From monastics in the Himalayas to urban professionals in the West, Buddhist practices have enabled people to cultivate self-discipline, compassion, and equanimity. The global popularity of Vipassana retreats, Zen training, and mindfulness workshops reflects this impact on personal lives.

2. Social Harmony and Conflict Resolution

Buddhist principles have been applied to resolve social and ethnic conflicts. For instance:

In Sri Lanka, Buddhist monks have initiated peacebuilding efforts after years of civil war.

In Myanmar, though controversial in recent years, traditional Buddhist values still guide interfaith harmony initiatives.

In Thailand, meditation is being introduced in prisons, reforming inmates and reducing repeat offenses.

In the West, Buddhist centers are becoming safe spaces for community healing and spiritual dialogue.

Buddhism's emphasis on non-judgmental listening, patience, and forgiveness has made it a powerful tool in reconciliation processes.

3. Interfaith Dialogue and Global Ethics

Buddhism plays a key role in promoting interreligious understanding. The Dalai Lama, a global ambassador of peace, has long advocated dialogue between religions, stressing that all faiths aim at alleviating human suffering.

Buddhism's non-dogmatic nature allows it to coexist peacefully with other belief systems. This openness has encouraged collaborative platforms for religious tolerance and global ethical discussions, especially around climate change, peace, and social justice.

4. Influence on Art, Architecture, and Literature

Buddhism has inspired centuries of creativity – from Ajanta and Ellora cave paintings to Zen gardens in Japan, from haiku poetry to modern mindfulness-themed fiction. Its aesthetic of simplicity, balance, and stillness has deeply influenced global art and architecture.

Today, Buddhist motifs are found in interior design, films, music, and even technology design (like minimalist user interfaces influenced by Zen aesthetics).

5. Contribution to Psychology and Neuroscience

Modern science has increasingly acknowledged what Buddhism has known for centuries. Research in neuroscience shows that meditation reshapes the brain – enhancing emotional regulation, attention, and empathy.

Buddhist teachings on impermanence, detachment, and awareness have informed:

- Cognitive-behavioral therapy (CBT)
- Dialectical behavior therapy (DBT)
- Acceptance and commitment therapy (ACT)

These modern therapies owe a debt to Buddhist psychology's profound insights into the mind.

6. Environmental Ethics

Long before "sustainability" became a buzzword, Buddhism taught respect for all life forms. The idea of dependent origination fosters a deep ecological awareness – emphasizing that humans are not separate from nature but part of an interconnected web.

Today, many Buddhist communities actively participate in tree-planting, wildlife protection, and climate advocacy. The concept of "engaged Buddhism", coined by Vietnamese monk Thich Nhat Hanh, calls on Buddhists to take compassionate action for environmental and social justice.

7. Role in Education and Leadership

Buddhist ethics are finding their way into educational and leadership models. Concepts like right speech, right intention, and right livelihood guide ethical leadership in corporate, political, and educational settings.

Mindfulness programs in schools help children manage emotions and focus better, while business leaders are embracing conscious capitalism and mindful leadership inspired by Buddhist values.

FINAL THOUGHTS: A GENTLE FORCE SHAPING THE FUTURE

Though Buddhism does not seek to convert or dominate, its influence continues to spread – not by force, but by quiet example. Its impact lies not in loud declarations, but in the countless lives transformed by a gentle shift in perspective – from ego to empathy, from noise to stillness, from fear to peace.

As the world stumbles under the weight of its own excess, the message of the Buddha – to awaken, to be kind, to be free – rings louder than ever. Whether one follows Buddhism as a religion or simply draws from its wisdom, its relevance in shaping a more balanced, peaceful, and compassionate world is undeniable.

> 'Thousands of candles can be lit from a single candle, and the life of the candle will not be shortened. Happiness never decreases by being shared.'
>
> – The Buddha

10

BRIEF CONCEPTUAL INTERPRETATION OF SOME IMPORTANT TERMS

A number of important terms are given below with a brief conceptual interpretation.

Abhidharma Pitaka: The term simply means 'higher Dharma', or 'higher teachings'. It is a systematic attempt to define The Buddha's teachings and understand their interrelationships. One of the three baskets of Buddhist sacred texts. *Abhidharma Pitaka* is an analytical writing interpreting the philosophy Buddhism deals with. The basket of text deals with the discourses from the life and teachings of the Buddha several centuries after his death.

Abhijjha: *Abhijja* comes from *abhi* + *iccha,* or strong craving or attachment. It is covetousness, acquisitiveness, desire for what one does not have. The root cause of all suffering is extreme greed or *abhijja*. The term is synonymous with craving (*trsna*) and desire (*lobha*).

Abhinna: It is a Buddhist term meaning direct knowledge. It may also mean 'higher knowledge' or 'supernormal knowledge'. In Buddhism, such special knowledge is obtained through virtuous living and meditation. The attainment of the four *jhanas*, or meditative absorptions, is considered a prerequisite for their attainment.

Abrahmacariya: That which is contrary to the pure life, which naturally would be interpreted as essentially consisting in the breakage of one of the precepts, especially by engaging in sexual intercourse.

Abyapada: Non-ill-will, absence of malevolence.

Adhicittasikkha: (adhi+citta+sikkhā) It means training in higher mind. There are three training – *adicittashikkha*, *adhipannasikkha* (training in higher wisdom or insight and adhisilasikkha (training in higher virtue). They are referred to as 'ascetic tasks of an ascetic'. It consists of a thorough undertaking of the Patimokkha's rules, at AN 3. 93 that they are 'urgent tasks of a *bhikkhu*' and at AN 6. 30 that they constitute the 'supreme training' (*anuttariyam sikkha*) for the purification of beings, etc.

Agama: The *Agamas*, which means 'which has come down', are a collection of several Tantric literature and scriptures of Hindu schools. The canonical texts there are of three – Shaiva, Vaishnava and Shakta. Some Agamas are Vedic and others non-Vedic. Epigraphical and archaeological evidence suggests that Agama texts were in existence by about the middle of the 1st millennium CE.

In Buddhism, an *Agama* is a collection of early Buddhist texts. The *Suttapitaka* of the early Buddhist schools has the five Agama together.

Of the four *Agamas* in the Chinese Buddhist Canon, the *Ekottara Agama* contains variants in the teachings of the Noble Eightfold Path and there is considerable disparity between the Pali and the (Chinese) versions. The other *Ksudraka Agama* or 'Minor Collection' corresponds to the *Khuddaka Nikaya*, and existed in some schools.

Ahimsa: It is the devotion to non-violence and respect for all forms of life. Practisers of ahimsa are often vegetarians or vegans

In Buddhist texts ahimsa is part of the Five Precepts (*Pancasila*), the first of which has been to abstain from killing. This precept of ahimsa is applicable to both the Buddhist layperson and the monastic community.

The ahimsa precept is not a commandment, and transgressions did not invite religious sanctions for laypersons, but their power has been in the Buddhist belief in karmic consequences and their impact in afterlife during rebirth.

Akshobhya: Akshobhya is one of the Five Wisdom Buddhas, a product of the Adibuddha, who represents consciousness as an aspect of reality. By convention he is located in the east of the Diamond Realm and is the lord of the Eastern Pure Land *Abhirati* (The Joyous). His consort is Lochana and he is normally accompanied by two elephants. His colour is blue-black and his attributes include a bell, three robes, and staff, as well as a jewel, lotus, prayer wheel, and sword. He has several emanations.

Amitabha: *Amitabha* is a Sanskrit word that means 'Infinite Light' Buddha. It is a Pure Land (*Sukhavati*) Buddhism. Pure Land Buddhists do not need to participate in meditation or become ascetics. Instead, they need only have faith in the *Amida* Buddha and recite his name with gratitude and reverence. Amitava's followers will be reborn in the pure land (*Sukhavati*) when they die.

Amoghasiddhi: *Amoghasiddhi* is one of the Five Wisdom Buddhas of the Mahayana and Vajrayana tradition of Buddhism. He is associated with the accomplishment of the Buddhist path and of the destruction of the poison of envy. His name means Unfailing Accomplishment. His consort is Tara, meaning Liberator and his mounts are garudas. He belongs to the family of *karma* whose family symbol is the double *vajra*.

***Anagami* (Non-returner):** A being when he will attain *nirvana*, will never return to this world. He has overcome the five hindrances that bind the mind to *samsara*, the cycle of rebirth, and so, after death, he will reach the Pure Abodes from where he will never return to this world.

Anagarika: In Buddhism, an *Anagarika* (Pali, 'homeless one' is a person who has given up most or all of their worldly possessions and responsibilities to commit full-time to Buddhist practice. It is a midway status between a *bhikkhu* or *bhikkhuni* (fully ordained monastics) and laypersons. An *Anagarika* takes the Eight Precepts, and might remain in this state for life.

Notable *Anagarikas* are –

- *Anagarika Dharmapal*
- *Anagarika Govinda*
- *Anagarika Munindra*
- *Anagarika Prajnananda*
- *Anagarika Dhammadinna*

Anatta: It is the denial of the soul in any phenomena. Buddhist philosophy has strongly advocated the way of denial or negation, beginning with the Buddha's own theory of *anatta* (not-atman, not-self) which denies any truly existent and unchanging essence of a person. Madhyamaka is a Buddhist philosophical school founded by Nagarjuna (2nd–3rd century AD), which is based on a fourfold negation of all assertions and concepts and promotes the theory of emptiness (shunyata). Apophatic assertions are also an important feature of Mahayana *sutras*, especially the prajnaparamita genre. These currents of negative theology are visible in all forms of Buddhism.

Anicca: Anicca is the Pali word meaning impermanence (non-nicca or non-permanent). The concept of impermanence is prominent in Buddhism, and it is also found in various schools of Hinduism and Jainism. The term also appears in the *Rigveda*.

According to Buddhism, living beings go through many births. Buddhism does not teach the existence of a permanent, immutable soul. The birth of one form from another is part of a process of continuous change. In other words, all are temporal things, whether material or mental, and are subject to decline and destruction.

Appamada: Heedfulness; diligence; zeal. The cornerstone of all skillful mental states, and one of such fundamental import that the Buddha stressed it in his parting words to his disciples: 'All fabrications are subject to decay. Bring about completion by being heedful!'

Arhat: One who has attained the goal of enlightenment or awakening (*bodhi*). An Arhat is free of the ten fetters (*samyojana*), and on death is not reborn. The difference between an Arhat and a Buddha is that the Buddha attains enlightenment by himself, whereas the Arhat does it by following the teachings of another.

As taught in early Buddhism. The Arhat attains exactly the same goal as the Buddha. Mahayana Buddhists criticize the arhat ideal on the grounds that the bodhisattva is a higher goal of perfection, for the bodhisattva vows to become a buddha in order to work for the good of others. This divergence of opinion continues to be one of the fundamental differences between the Theravada and Mahayana traditions.

***Avalokiteshvara*:** In Buddhism, *Avalokitesvara* means the lord who looks down. He is also known as *Lokesvara* (Lord of the World). He is often associated with Amitabha Buddha. Avalokitesvara has numerous manifestations and is depicted in various forms and styles.

***Bardo*:** Tibetan term for the period between death and rebirth.

Bhagava: The blessed one, another name for the Buddha.

***Bhante* (Vante):** Venerable sir. A Sri Lankan term often used when addressing a Theravada Buddhist monk.

***Bhavacakra*:** The bhavacakra is found on the walls of Tibetan Buddhist temples and monasteries in the Indo-Tibetan region, to help both Buddhists and non-Buddhists understand the core Buddhist teachings. The image consists of four concentric circles, held by Yama, the lord of Death, with an image of the Buddha pointing to the moon metaphysically representing the possibility for liberation from the suffering of reincarnation.

Bhavachakra or 'wheel of life' consists of the words bhava and chakra. In Buddhism, bhava denotes the continuity of becoming and Chakra meaning 'wheel' or 'circle' or yantras.

***Bhikkhu*:** A *bhikkhu* or *bhiksu* is an ordained male in Buddhist monasticism. Female monastics are *bhikkhuni* (nun). They are also members of the *Sangha* (Buddhist community).

Bodhi: The term bodhi acquired a variety of meanings and connotations during the development of Buddhist thoughts in the various schools.

Bodhi means Awakening or Enlightenment. In early Buddhism, bodhi carried a meaning synonymous to nirvana to describe the insight, which implied the extinction of *lobha* (greed), *dosa* (hate) and *moha* (delusion).

In Theravada Buddhism, bodhi and nirvana carry the same meaning: that of being freed from greed, hate and delusion. Bodhi, specifically, refers to the realisation of the four stages of enlightenment and becoming an Arahat. It is equal to supreme insight, the realisation of the four noble truths, which leads to deliverance. Attaining nirvana is the ultimate goal of Theravada and other sravakas traditions. It involves the abandonment of the ten fetters and the cessation of *dukkha* or suffering.

In Mahayana-thought, bodhi is the realization of the inseparability of samsara and nirvana.

Mahayana discerns three forms of awakened beings: a) Arahat–Liberation for oneself, b) Bodhisattva – Liberation for living beings, c) Full Buddhahood.

Bodhicitta: In Mahayana Buddhism, bodhicitta is enlightenment-mind. The mind (*citta*) is aimed at awakening (*bodhi*), with wisdom and compassion for the benefit of all sentient beings.

Bodhisattvas: In Buddhism, a bodhisattva is a person who is on the path towards bodhi ('awakening') or Buddhahood.

In the Early Buddhist schools, as well as modern Theravada Buddhism, bodhisattva refers to someone who has made a resolution to become a Buddha and has also received a confirmation or prediction from a living Buddha that this will be so.

In Mahayana Buddhism, a bodhisattva refers to anyone who has generated bodhicitta, a spontaneous wish and compassionate mind to attain Buddhahood for the benefit of all sentient beings.

List of Bodhisattvas

- ***Akasagarbha***: The Bodhisattva of infinite happiness generated by helping countless numbers of sentient beings. He manifests wisdom.
- ***Avalokitesvara***: The bodhisattva of compassion, the listener of the world's cries who uses skillful means to come to their aid; the most universally acknowledged Bodhisattva in Mahayana Buddhism. Known as Guan Yin in East Asia, Chenrezig in Tibet, and Migjid Janraisig in Mongolia. He is described as holding a lotus flower.
- ***Ksitigarbha***: It means Earth Womb. The bodhisattva of the beings suffering in hellish realms, or the bodhisattva of great vows. He is revered as the guardian of children and patron deity of deceased children.
- ***Mahasthamaprapta***: Represents the power of wisdom, seen on the left of Amitabha in Pure Land Buddhism.
- ***Maitreya***: Also known as Ajita Bodhisattva. The bodhisattva to be reborn and to become enlightened, thus succeeding Gautama Buddha in the future. Known for his benevolence. He keeps a Kumbha or phililal in his hand and is destined to rule Varanasi (Pure Land).
- ***Manjusri***: Bodhisattva of keen awareness and wisdom. Wields a flaming sword in his right hand
- ***Nagarjuna***: The founder of the Madhyamaka (Middle Path) school of Mahayana Buddhism.

- *Nio*: Two wrath-filled and muscular guardians of the Buddha, standing today at the entrance of many Buddhist temples in Japan and Korea under the appearance of frightening wrestler-like statues. They are manifestations of the Bodhisattva Vajrapani.
- ***Padmasambhava***: Most associated with Tibetan Buddhism and Bhutanese Buddhism. The Nyingma school regards Padmasambhava as a second Buddha.
- ***Samantabhadra***: Represents the practice and meditation of all Buddhas.
- ***Sangharama***: Only revered in Chinese Buddhism-Taoism, Sangharama refer to a group of devas who guard Buddhist monasteries and the faith, but the title is usually referring to the legendary Chinese military general Guan Yu, who became a Dharmapala through becoming a Buddhist and making vows.
- ***Sitatapatra***: The goddess of the White Parasol and protector against supernatural danger.
- ***Skanda***: A Dharmapala who guards the Dharma, with links to Vajrapani and is somewhat the direct forbear to Murugan, a Hindu deity. Primarily worshipped in Chinese Buddhism.
- ***Supushpachandra***: One of two attendants of Bhaisajyaguru Buddha.
- ***Tara***: Female bodhisattva, or set of bodhisattvas, in Tibetan Buddhism. She represents the virtues of success in work and achievements. Also, a manifestation of Avalokitesvara.
- ***Vajrapani***: He is described as one of the 3 protective deities around Buddha, other are Manjusri and Avlokiteshwara. Vajrapani manifests Buddha's power while Buddha's

wisdom is manifested Buddha's wisdom and Avlokiteshwara manifests Buddha's compassion.

- *Vasudhara*: Bodhisattva of abundance and fertility. Popular in Nepal.

Cetana: As Bhikkhu Bodhi states, *Cetana* is the mental factor that is concerned with the actualization of a goal, that is, the conative or volitional aspect of cognition. The *Abhidharma-samuccaya* states *chetana* as a mental activity that propels the mind forward. It has the function of making the mind settle on what is positive, negative, or indeterminate.

Dependent origination: *Pratigyasamuppada* is commonly translated as dependent origination. It is a key doctrine in Buddhism shared by all schools of Buddhism. It states that all dharmas (phenomena) arise in dependence upon other dharmas: 'if this exists, that exists; if this ceases to exist, that also ceases to exist'. The basic principle is that all things (dharmas, phenomena, principles) arise in dependence upon other things.

Deva: A *Deva* in Buddhism is a type of celestial being or God who shares the god-like characteristics of being more powerful, longer-lived, and, in general, much happier than humans, although the same level of veneration is not paid to them as to Buddhas.

In East Asian Buddhism, the word deva is translated as 'heavenly person'. The feminine equivalent of deva, devi, is sometimes translated as 'heavenly female'. In Buddhist cosmology, 'Deva' refers to a class of beings or a path of the six paths of the incarnation cycle. It includes some very different types of beings which can be ranked hierarchically according to the merits they have accumulated over lifetimes. The lowest classes of these beings are closer in their nature to human beings than to the higher classes of deva. Devas can be degraded to humans or the beings in the three evil paths once they have consumed their merits.

***Dhammapada*:** *Dhammapada* is a collection of sayings of the Buddha in verse form and one of the most widely read and best-known Buddhist scriptures. The original version of the *Dhammapada* is in the *Khuddaka Nikaya*, a division of the Pali Canon of Theravada Buddhism.

Dharma (dhamma): the teachings of the Buddha.

***Dharmakaya*:** Buddha-mind, the pervasive essence

***Dharmapala*:** A *Dharmapala* is a type of wrathful god in Buddhism. The name means 'Dharma protector or defender' in Sanskrit, and the *Dharmapalas* are also known as the Defenders of the Law (Dharma), or the Protectors of the Law. There are two kinds of *Dharmapala*, Worldly Protectors and Wisdom Protectors. Only Wisdom Protectors are enlightened beings.

***Dipankara*:** Dipankara is one of the Buddhas of the past. He is said to have lived on Earth one hundred thousand aeons ago. According to some Buddhist traditions, Dipankara was a Buddha who reached enlightenment eons prior to Gautama Buddha, the historical Buddha.

Generally, Buddhists believe that there has been a succession of many Buddhas in the distant past and that many more will appear in the future; Dipankara, then, would be one of numerous previous Buddhas, while Gautama was the most recent, and Maitreya will be the next Buddha in the future.

***Dukkha*:** Suffering (*Dukkha*) Buddha describes, Birth is suffering, Aging is suffering. Illness is suffering, Death is suffering, Union with what is displeasing is suffering, Separation from what is pleasing is suffering, Not to get what one wants is suffering.

In brief, the five aggregates (which you learn soon) subject to clinging are suffering.

- **Origin of suffering (*Samudaya*):** Samudaya explains the origin of suffering. It is this craving (tanha) which leads to re-becoming, accompanied by delight and lust, seeking delight here and there; craving for sensual pleasures, craving for becoming, and craving for non-becoming.
- **Cessation of suffering (*Nirodha*):** Nirodha is acceptance of the cessation of suffering. It is the remainder less fading away and cessation of the craving (*tanha*), the giving up and relinquishing of it, freedom from it, non-reliance on it. The path leading to cessation (*Marga*).

This is the way leading to the cessation of suffering (*nirvana*). It is this noble eightfold path or middle path achieving right view, right intention, right speech, right action, right livelihood, right effort, right mindfulness, right concentration.

Four Noble Truths: The Four Noble Truths refer to and express the basic orientation of Buddhism. This is the four pillars the principle of nirvana rests on. The four truths describe *dukkha* and its ending as a means to reach peace of mind in this life, but also as a means to end rebirth.

Hinayana: Hinayana is a Sanskrit term that appeared around the first or second century. Hinayana is considered as the preliminary or small (hina) vehicle (yana) of the Buddha's teachings. It is often contrasted with Mahayana, the second vehicle of the Buddha's teachings, or the great (*maha*) vehicle (*yana*). The third vehicle of the Buddha's teachings is the *Vajrayana*, the indestructible (vajra) vehicle (yana).

Western scholars used the term Hinayana to describe the early teachings of Buddhism, as the Mahayana teachings were generally given later.

Jhana: Mental absorption. A state of strong concentration focused on a single physical sensation (resulting in *rupa jhana*) or mental notion (resulting in *Arupa jhana*). Development of *jhana* arises from the temporary suspension of the five hindrances through the development of five mental factors: *vitakka* (directed thought), *vicara* (evaluation), *piti* (rapture), *sukha* (pleasure), and *ekaggatarammana* (singleness of preoccupation).

Kakusandha Buddha: Kakusandha Buddha (Pali), is one of the ancient Buddhas whose biography is chronicled in Buddhavamsa, one of the books of the Pali Canon. According to Theravada Buddhist tradition, Kakusandha is the twenty-fifth of the twenty-nine named Buddhas, the fourth of the Seven Buddhas of Antiquity, and the first of the five Buddhas of the present *Kalpa*.

Kalpa: Kalpa is the period of time between the creation and recreation of a world or universe. In the Pali language of early Buddhism, the word takes the form kappa, and is mentioned in the assumed oldest scripture of Buddhism, the *Sutta Nipata*. The present *Kalpa* is called the *Bhadra Kalpa* (Auspicious aeon). The five Buddhas of the present *Kalpa* are:

- Kakusandha (the first Buddha of the bhadrakalpa)
- Koṇāgamana (the second Buddha of the bhadrakalpa)
- Kassapa (the third Buddha of the bhadrakalpa)
- Gautama (the fourth and present Buddha of the bhadrakalpa)

- Maitreya (the fifth and future Buddha of the bhadrakalpa)

Karma: *Karma* is a Sanskrit term that literally means 'action' or 'doing'. In the Buddhist tradition, *karma* refers to action driven by intention (cetana) which leads to future consequences. Those intentions are considered to be the determining factor in the kind of rebirth in samsara, the cycle of rebirth.

Kumbhanda: A Kumbhanda (Sanskrit) or Kumbhanda (Pali) is one of a group of dwarfish, misshapen spirits among the lesser deities of Buddhist mythology. The terms Kumbhanda and yaksa are sometimes used for the same person.

Madhyamaka: The Madhyamaka school of Buddhism, the followers of which are called Madhyamikas, was one of the two principal schools of Mahayana Buddhism in India, the other school being the Yogacara. The name of the school is a reference to the claim made of Buddhism in general that it is a middle path (madhyama pratipad) that avoids the two extremes of eternalism. This practice was founded by the Indian philosopher Nagarjuna. Madhyamaka also refers to the ultimate nature of phenomena and the realization of this in meditative equipoise.

Madhyamika: Madhyamika is the 'middle way' or 'centrism' which refers to a tradition of Buddhist philosophy and practice founded by the Indian Buddhist monk and philosopher Nagarjuna (c. 150 – c. 250 CE). The foundational text of the Madhyamika tradition is Nagarjuna's *Mulamadhyamakakarika* ('Root Verses on the Middle Way').

Mahabhuti: In Buddhism, the four Great Elements (Pali: cattaro mahabhutani) are earth, water, fire and air. *Mahabhuta* is generally synonymous with *catudhatu*, which is Pali for the 'Four Elements'.

Mahakyashapa: The monk who understood the silent sermon and led the first council.

***Mahamudra*:** Mahamudra literally means 'great seal' or 'great imprint' and refers to the fact that 'all phenomena inevitably are stamped by the fact of wisdom and emptiness inseparable'.

Maitreya: Maitreya is a bodhisattva who is regarded as the future Buddha of this world in all schools of Buddhism, prophesied to become Maitreya Buddha. It is also known as Ajita Bodhisattva.

Mandala: A complex, circular, symmetrical image used in meditation.

Mara: The personification of evil and temptation.

***Metta*:** Loving-kindness; goodwill. One of the ten perfections (paramis) and one of the four 'sublime abodes' (brahma-vihara).

***Mudita*:** Sympathetic joy, being happy for others, without a trace of envy. One of the four brahma vihara.

***Nekkhamma*:** Nekkhamma is a Pali word generally translated as 'renunciation' or "the pleasure of renunciation" while also conveying more specifically 'giving up the world and leading a holy life' or 'freedom from lust, craving and desires'. In Buddhism's Noble Eightfold Path, Nekkhamma is the first practice associated with 'Right Intention'. In the Theravada list of ten perfections, Nekkhamma is the third practice of 'perfection'. It involves non-attachment (detachment).

Nirvana: Nirvana is the highest state that someone can attain, a state of enlightenment, meaning a person's individual desires and suffering go away. The origin of the word nirvana relates to religious enlightenment; it comes from the Sanskrit meaning 'extinction, disappearance' of the individual to the universal.

***Pabbajja*:** Pabbajja (Pali; Sanskrit. : pravrajya) literally means 'to go forth' and refers to when a layperson leaves home to live the life of a Buddhist renunciate among a community of *bhikkhus* (fully ordained monks). This generally involves preliminary ordination as a novice (m. Samanera, f. Samaneri). It is sometimes referred to as 'lower ordination'. After a period or when the novice reaches 20 years of age, the novice can be considered for the Upasampada ordination (or 'higher ordination') whereby the novice becomes a monk (*bhikkhu*) or nun (*bhikkhuni*).

***Papanca*:** Complication, proliferation. The tendency of the mind to proliferate issues from the sense of 'self'. This term can also be translated as self-reflexive thinking, reification, falsification, distortion, elaboration, or exaggeration. In the discourses, it is frequently used in analyses of the psychology of conflict.

Paramartha: Paramartha (499-569 CE) was an Indian monk from Ujjain in central India, who is best known for his prolific Chinese translations which include Vasubandhu's Abhidharmakosa. Paramartha is considered one of the greatest translators of *sutras* in Chinese Buddhism, along with Kumarajiva and Xuanzang.

***Parami*:** Perfection of the character. A group of ten qualities developed over many lifetimes by a Bodhisatta, which appear as a group in the Pali Canon only in the *Jataka* (Birth Stories): generosity (*Dana*), virtue (*Sila*), renunciation (*Nekkhamma*), discernment (*Panna*), energy/persistence (*Viriya*), patience/forbearance (*Khanti*), truthfulness (*Sacca*), determination (*Adhitthana*), good will (*Metta*), and equanimity (*Upekkha*).

***Paramita*:** Paramita (Sanskrit, Pali) or parami (Pali), is a Buddhist term often translated as 'perfection'. It is described in Buddhist commentaries as noble character qualities generally associated with enlightened beings.

***Parinirvana*:** In Buddhism, *parinirvana* (Sanskrit: *Parinirvana*; Pali: Parinibbana) is commonly used to refer to nirvana-after-death, which occurs upon the death of someone who has attained nirvana during his or her lifetime. It implies a release from the Samsara, *karma* and rebirth as well as the dissolution of the skandhas. In some Mahayana scriptures, notably the Mahayana *Mahaparinirvana Sutra*, *Parinirvana* is described as the realm of the eternal true Self of the Buddha.

***Piti*:** Rapture; bliss; delight. In meditation, a pleasurable quality in the mind that reaches full maturity upon the development of the second level of *jhana*.

***Prajna*:** Prajna (Sanskrit) or panna (Pali), is a Buddhist term often translated as 'wisdom', 'intelligence', or 'understanding'. It is described in Buddhist commentaries as the understanding of the true nature of phenomena. In the context of Buddhist meditation, it is the ability to understand the three characteristics of all things: *anicca* (impermanence), *dukkha* (dissatisfaction or suffering), and *anatta* (non-self). Mahayana texts describe it as the understanding of *shunyata* (emptiness). It is part of the Threefold Training in Buddhism, and is one of the ten paramis of Theravada Buddhism and one of the six Mahayana paramitas.

***Prajnaparamita*:** A massive collection of Mahayana texts, including the Heart and Diamond *Sutras*.

***Pratityasamutpada*:** It is the theory of dependent origination, which literally means 'arising on the ground of a preceding cause', could well be considered the common denominator of all

Buddhist traditions throughout the world, whether Theravada, Mahayana, or Vajrayana.

Pratyekabuddha: In the early tradition of the Pali canon the pratyekabuddha refers to a male individual who has attained enlightenment or insight (bodhi; hence, buddha) by himself. In contrast to a Samma Sambuddha (Sanskrit, Samyak sambuddha), which is a completely enlightened person, a pratyekabuddha keeps enlightenment for himself (pratyeka) and does not embark on a career of preaching it to others.

Ratnasambhava: Ratnasambhava or 'Jewel-Born' is one of the Five Dhyani Buddhas or 'Five Meditation Buddhas' of Mahayana and Vajrayana or Tantric Buddhism. Ratnasambhava's mandalas and mantras focus on developing equanimity and equality and, in Vajrayana Buddhist thought is associated with the attempt to destroy greed and pride. His consort is Mamaki and his mount is a horse or a pair of lions. Ratnasaṃbhava is associated with the skandha of feeling or sensation and its relationship with consciousness. His activity in promoting Buddhism is enriching and increasing knowledge of Dharma. Ratnasambhava is associated with the jewel symbol, which corresponds with his family, Ratna or jewel. In artwork he is shown in the *mudra* of giving.

Rinpoche: (rin-po-che) literally means 'precious one', and may *refer* to a person, place, or thing – like the word's 'gem' or 'jewel'. The word consists of *rin* (value), *po* (nominalizing suffix) and *chen* (big). The word is used in the context of Tibetan Buddhism as a way of showing respect when addressing those recognized as reincarnated, older, respected, notable, learned and an accomplished Lamas or teachers of the Dharma.

Saddha: Conviction, faith. A confidence in the Buddha that gives one the willingness to put his teachings into practice. Conviction becomes unshakeable upon the attainment of stream-entry.

Samadhi: Concentration; the practice of centring the mind in a single sensation or preoccupation, usually to the point of *jhana*.

Samanera: Samanera is a male novice monk, who will be considered for the higher *Bhikkhu* ordination after a year or until the ripe age of 20. He is one who is making a first approach to full membership of the Buddhist *sangha*.

Samatha: Samatha refers to mental stabilization. It is tranquil meditation which is distinguished from *vipassana* meditation. The *Abhidhamma Pitaka* and the commentaries describe Samatha and vipassana as two separate techniques, taking Samatha to mean concentration-meditation, and vipassana as a practice to gain insight. In the Theravada tradition, vipassana is a practice that seeks 'insight into the true nature of reality', which is defined as anicca (impermanence), *dukkha* (suffering, unsatisfactoriness), and *anatta* (non-self): the three marks of existence. In the Mahayana traditions vipassana is defined as insight into *sunyata* (emptiness) and Buddha-nature.

Sambhogakaya: Buddha as a deva or God.

Samjna: Perception

Samsara: Samsara, in Buddhism and Hinduism is the beginningless cycle of repeated birth, mundane existence and dying again. Samsara is considered to be *dukkha*, suffering, and in general unsatisfactory and painful, perpetuated by desire and *avidya* (ignorance), and the resulting *karma*.

In several *suttas* of the Samyutta Nikaya it's said, it is the never-ending repetitive cycle of birth and death, in six realms of reality (gati, domains of existence), wandering from one life to another life with no particular direction or purpose. Every rebirth is temporary and impermanent. In each rebirth one is born, and dies, to be reborn elsewhere in accordance with one's own *karma*. It is perpetuated by one's *avidya* (ignorance), particularly about *anicca* (impermanence) and *anatta*, (no-self), and from craving. Samsara continues until moksha is attained by means of insight and nirvana.

Samvriti: In Buddhist context, samvriti refers to the conventional, as opposed to absolute, truth or reality. Knowledge is considered as split into three levels: the first being the illusory (called *samvriti*, *parikalpita* or *pratibhasika* according to different schools of thought), considered false compared to the empirical (*samvriti*, *paratantra* or *vyavaharika*), in turn trumped by the transcendental (*paramartha* or *paramarthika*).

Sangha: In Buddhism, *sangha* refers to the monastic community of *bhikkhus* (monks) and *bhikkhunis* (nuns).

Shakyamuni: Sage of the Sakyas, a name for the Buddha.

Sikhi: According to the Buddhavamsa and Buddhist mythology, Sikhi is the twenty-third of twenty-eight Buddhas. The penultimate Buddha of the *Alamkarakalpa* (Adorned Eon), Sikhi was preceded by *Vipassi* Buddha and succeeded by Vessabhu Buddha.

Tanha: Tanha is an important concept in Buddhism, that refers to 'thirst, desire, longing, greed', either physical or mental. It is typically translated as craving. Tanha is of three types: Kama-tanha (craving for sensual pleasures), Bhava-Tanha (craving for existence), and Vibhava-Tanha (craving for non-existence). Tanha appears in the Four Noble Truths.

Tathagata: *Tathagata* is a Pali and Sanskrit word which is used by Gautama Buddha when referring to himself or other Buddhas in the Pali Canon. Likewise, in the Mahayana corpus, it is an epithet of Shakyamuni Buddha and the other celestial buddhas. The term is often thought to mean either 'one who has thus gone' (*Tathagata*), 'one who has thus come' (*Tathagata*), or sometimes 'one who has thus not gone' (*Tathagata*). This is interpreted as signifying that the *Tathagata* is beyond all coming and going – beyond all transitory phenomena.

There are, however, other interpretations.

Tatha means 'thus' in Sanskrit and Pali, and Buddhist thought takes this to refer to what is called 'reality as-it-is' (*yathabhuta*).

Another interpretation, proposed by the scholar Richard Gombrich, is that *Tathagata* is likely to mean 'one like that', with no motion in either direction. More interpretations are there.

In Vajrayana Buddhism, the Five *Tathagata* are the Five Great Buddhas, which is associated with the *Dharmakaya* (dharma-body) which embodies the principle of enlightenment in Buddhism. In a Vairocana mandala, the Buddhas are arranged like this: *Amoghasiddhi* (North), *Amitabha* (West), *Vairocana* (Principal deity/ meditator), *Akshobhya* (East) and *Ratnasambhava* (South).

Three Jewels: Three Jewels is also known as the Triple Gem or Three Refuges. In Pali it is *ti-ratana* or *ratana-ttaya* which are the Buddha, the Dharma, and the *Sangha*. Three Jewels is known as the Triple Gem or Three Refuges.

Trailokya: *Trailokya* has been translated as 'three worlds' 'three spheres', 'three planes of existence', 'three realms' and 'three regions'.

In Buddhism, the three worlds refer to the following destinations for karmic rebirth:

- ***Kamaloka***: the world of desire, typified by base desires, populated by hell beings, *preta*, animals, ghosts, humans and lower demi-gods.
- ***Rupaloka***: the world of form, predominately free of baser desires, populated by dhyana-dwelling gods, possible rebirth destination for those well practiced in dhyāna.
- ***Arupaloka***: the world of formlessness, a noncorporeal realm populated with four heavens, possible rebirth destination for practitioners of the four formlessness stages.

Tulku: A *Tulku* is a reincarnate custodian of a specific lineage of teachings in Tibetan Buddhism who is given empowerments and trained from a young age by students of his or her predecessor. Examples of tulkus include the Dalai Lamas.

Upadana: *Upadana* is a Sanskrit and Pali word that means 'fuel, material cause, substrate that is the source and means for keeping an active process energized'. It is also an important Buddhist concept referring to 'attachment, clinging, grasping'. It is considered to be the result of *tanha* (craving), and is part of the *dukkha* (dissatisfaction, suffering, pain) doctrine in Buddhism.

Upasampada: *Upasampada* literally denotes 'approaching or nearing the ascetic tradition'. In more common parlance it specifically refers to the rite and ritual of ascetic vetting (ordination) by which a candidate, if deemed acceptable, enters the community as *upasampadan* (ordained) and is authorized to undertake ascetic life.

Vairocana: *Vairocana* (from Sanskrit: Vi+rocana, 'from the sun' or 'belonging to the sun', 'Solar', or 'Shining') also known as *Mahavairocana* (Great Vairocana) is a major Buddha from

Mahayana and Vajrayana Buddhism. [1] Vairocana is often interpreted, in texts like the *Avatamsaka Sutra*, as the Dharmakaya [2][3][4] of the historical Gautama Buddha.

The Spring Temple Buddha, a colossal statue of Vairocana, in Lushan County, Henan, China. It has a total height of 153 meters (502 ft), including the 25-meter (82 ft) lotus throne which the statue stands on.

In East Asian Buddhism (Chinese, Korean, Japanese and Vietnamese Buddhism), Vairocana is also seen as the dharmakaya (the supreme buddha-body, the body of ultimate reality), and the embodiment of the Buddhist concept of wisdom and purity. [5] Mahavairocana is often translated into east Asian languages as 'Great Sun Buddha' Buddha. In the conception of the Five Jinas of Mahayana and Vajrayana Buddhism, Vairocana is at the centre and is often considered a Primordial Buddha. In east Asian Esoteric Buddhism, Mahavairocana is considered to be a cosmic Buddha whose body is the entire universe, the Dharmadhatu.

Vajrapani: The name '*Vajrapani*' originates from the Sanskrit words 'Vajra', meaning thunderbolt or diamond, and 'Pani', signifying hand. Hence, Vajrapani is commonly known as the 'Holder of the Thunderbolt' or the 'Diamond Hand'. It is revered as the 'Indestructible Hand of Buddha'. It holds a prominent and powerful position in Buddhist cosmology. The thunderbolt symbolizes an unshakable and indestructible force, reflecting the unwavering strength of Vajrapani. Depicted with a fierce expression, Vajrapani's wrathful aspect represents his role in overcoming obstacles and dispelling ignorance.

Vajrapani is closely associated with the practice of tantra, a form of esoteric Buddhism that emphasizes ritual and meditative techniques. As a bodhisattva, Vajrapani bodhisattva has voluntarily delayed his own enlightenment to guide and assist others on their spiritual path.

The embodiment of the power of all the Buddhas. He appears in a wrathful aspect, displaying his power to overcome outer, inner, and secret obstacles. At the time of Buddha Shakyamuni, he manifested as a Bodhisattva disciple in order to show Buddha's disciples how to be perfect Mahayana disciples.

Vasubandhu: He was a great Indian Buddhist scholar of the fifth century who was converted to the Mahayana by his older brother, Asanga. He wrote the Treasury of Abhidharma (*Abhidharmakosha*).

***Vihara*:** Literally, 'dwelling' or 'refuge', the Buddhist monastery. Initially, it was a shelter for the rainy season only, but in time came to be a permanent home for a *sangha*. The construction of a vihara is usually undertaken by a wealthy benefactor, rather than as an act of the *sangha* itself. As a result, many are beautiful examples of architecture.

Zen: Zen is a school of Mahayana Buddhism that originated in China during the Tang dynasty as the Chan School or the Buddha-mind school and later developed into various sub-schools and branches. Zen was influenced by Taoism, especially Neo-Daoist thought, and developed as a distinguished school of Chinese Buddhism. From China, Chan spread south to Vietnam and became Vietnamese Thien, northeast to Korea to become Seon Buddhism, and east to Japan, becoming Japanese Zen.

BIBLIOGRAPHY

REFERENCES

Chapter One

(1-1): Rupert Gethin, *The Foundations of Buddhism* (New York: Oxford University Press, 1998).

(1-2): Maurice Bloomfield, Monier Monier-Williams, Ernst Leumann, and Carl Cappeller, *A Sanskrit-English Dictionary, Etymologically and Philologically Arranged with Special Reference to Cognate Indo-European Languages* (Motilal Banarsidass), 733.

(1-3): The Life or Legend of Gautama

(1-4): Translated into English by Rhys Davids as "Buddhist Birth Stories"

(1-5): Dr. Samir Kumar Datta, *Asvaghosa as a Poet and a Dramatist* (Burdwan University Publications).

(1-6): T. W. Rhys Davids, *Buddhism: Its History and Literature* (New York and London: G.P. Putnam's sons, 1896), 62.

(1-7): Edward B. Cowell, *The Buddha-Carita* (1893).

(1- 8): Trans. W. Woodville Kookhill, *The life of the Buddha and the early history of his order, derived from Tibetan works in the Bkah-Hgyur and*

Bstan-Hgyur, followed by notices on the early history of Tibet and Khoten, (London: Trubnek & Co., 1894).

(1-9): Bhikku Bodhi, *The Noble Search*. 26.

Chapter Two

(2-1): T. B. Karunaratne, *The Buddhist Wheel Symbol* (Sri Lanka: Buddhist Publication Society, 1969).

(2-2): Peter Harvey on *Dukkha, Non-Self, and the Teaching of the Four Noble Truths*, in Steven M. Emmanuel, A Companion to Buddhist Philosophy (1937), 30.

(2-3): *Craving and Dukkha*, by Bhikkhu Analayo.

(2-4): *The Nobility of the Truths* by Bhikkhu Bodhi

(2-5): Rupert Gethin, *The Cessation of Dukkha*, (2001), 190-226.

(2-6): *The Nobility of the Truths* by Bhikkhu Bodhi

(2-7): *Buddhist Precept and Practice*. (Delhi: Motilal Banarsidass, 1991.)

(2-8): Johannes Bronkhorst, *Buddhist Teaching in India*, (Simon and Schuster, 2009), 124-125.

(2-9): Steven Collins, *Selfless Persons: Imagery and Thought in Theravada Buddhism* (Cambridge University Press, 1990), 71-81.

Chapter Three

(3-1): Richard Salomon, Ancient Scrolls from Gandhara (The British Library).

(3-2): Sheng Yen Series, *Spreading Buddha's Word in East Asia: The Formation and Transformation of the Chinese Buddhist Canon* (Columbia University Press, 2016).

(3-3): *The Dawn of Abhidharma* by Bhikkhu Analayo.

(3-4): Jose Ignacio Cabezon, *Buddhist Studies as a Discipline and the Role of Theory* (Journal of the Internation Association of Buddhist Studies, Volume 18, Number 2, 1995), 233.

(3-5): LaMotte, *The History of Indian Buddhism*, 1988.

(3-6): Richard Gombrich, *What the Buddha Thought* (2009), 96.

Chapter Four

(4-1): Lecture on the Science of Religion- Max Muller, 1873.
(4-2): Wisdom of India - Lin Yu Tang)
(4-3): Conze Edward, *Buddhist Thoughts in India: Three Phases of Buddhist Philosophy*, (Rutledge, Volume 4, 2013).
(4-4): Bhikkhu Analayo, *The First Sangiti and Theravada Monasticism* (Sri Lanka International Journal of Buddhist Studies, Volume IV, 2015).
(4-5): The Early Buddhist Councils – Tricycle: The Buddhist Review
(4-6): The twelfth chapter of the Cullavagga (Vin. ii.)
(4-7): Charles Willemen, Bart Dessein, and Collet Cox, *Sarvastivada Buddhist Scholasticism* (Brill, Handbuch Der Orientalistik).

Chapter Five

(5-1): Berkwitz, Stephen C., *South Asian Buddhism: A Survey* (Routledge, 2012).
(5-2): *An Introduction to Buddhism: Teachings, History, and Practices* (Cambridge: Cambridge University Press, 2nd Ed).
(5-3): Charles Willemen, Bart Dessein, and Collet Cox, *Sarvastivada Buddhist Scholasticism* (Brill, Handbuch Der Orientalistik).
(5-4): K. L. Dhammajoti, *Sarvastivada Abhidharma*, (Centre of Buddhist Studies, The University of Hong Kong, 2009).

Chapter Six

(6-1): T. W. Rhys Davids, *Buddhism: Its History and Literature* (New York and London: G.P. Putnam's sons, 1896), 38.
(6-2): Bhikkhuni Patimokkha, *The Bhikkhunis' Code of Discipline* (translated from Pali by Thanissaro Bhikkhu).
(6-3): Trans. Rhys Davids & Hermann Oldenberg, *Vinaya Texts: Sacred Books of the East*, (Oxford: volumes XIII, XVII & XX, 1881).
(6-4): Trans. I. B. Horner, *The Book of the Discipline*, (Oxford: Pali Text Society, Volume VI, 1966).

(6-5): Maurice Walshe, *The Long Discourses of the Buddha: A Translation of the Digha Nikaya*, formerly titled: *Thus, Have I Heard* (Boston: Wisdom Publications, 1987).

(6-6): *Connected Discourses of the Buddha* by Bhikkhu Bodhi.

(6-7): *Befriending the Suttas: Tips on Reading the Pali Discourses*

(6-8): Talks, Writings and Translation by Thanissaro Bhikkhu, Dhammatalks.org.

(6-9): *Majjhima Nikaya: The Middle-length Discourses*, ed by Access to Insight, Access to Insight (BCBS Edition), 21 December 2013, http://www. accesstoinsight. org/tipitaka/mn/index.html.

(6-10): Bhikkhu Bodhi, *Connected Discourses of the Buddha* (Somerville: Wisdom Publications, 2000), 31.

(6-11): Rhys Davids, 43.

(6-12): Trans. Narada Maha Thera, *A Manual of Abhidhamma Bhadanta Anuruddhaacariya*, Edited in the original Pali text (Buddhist Missionary Soceity).

Chapter Seven

(7-1): T. W. Rhys Davids, *Vinaya: The Mahavagga (Part 2)* (Motilal Banarasidass, 2008).

(7-2): Johannes Bronkhorst, *Did the Buddha Believe in Karma and Rebirth?* (Journal of the International Association of Buddhist Studies, Volume 21, Number 1, 1998).

(7-3): Rhys Davids, 87-88.

(7-4): *Wisdom of India*, ed. Lin YuTang.

(7-5): Thanissaro Bhikkhu, *Vera Sutta: Animosity*, trans. from Pali, (AN 10.92 PTS: A v 182).

(7-6): *Cakkhu Sutta*. Translated by Bhikkhu, Thanissaro, dhamma talks. org. Retrieved 2023-04-29 – via Access to Insight. He is incapable of doing any deed by which he might be reborn in hell, in the animal womb, or in the realm of hungry ghosts. He is incapable of passing away until he has realized the fruit of stream-entry.

(7-7): *Bodhi Transcendental Dependent Arising*, a translation and exposition of the *Upanisa Sutta* by Bhikkhu Bodhi (1995).

Chapter Eight

(8-1): Rupert Gethin, *The Foundations of Buddhism*.

(8-2): David Drewes, *Early Indian Mahayan Buddhism II: News Perspectives, Religion Compass.*

(8-3): Martin Luther King Jr., *The Chief Characteristics and Doctrines of Mahayana Buddhism* (Standford: The Martin Luther King Jr. Research and Education Institute).

Chapter Nine

(9-1): Joseph Nye, *Bound to Lead: The Changing Nature of American Power* (1990).

(9-2): Bhaswati Sarmah Department of Political Science in a thesis submitted to Sikkim University, *A Study on the role of Buddhism in relations with Japan and Mongolia*.

(9-3) Shantanu Kishwar, *The Rising Role of Buddhism in India's Soft Power Strategy* (Issue Briefs, Aug 20, 2023).

(9-4): Daya Kishan Thussu, *Communication India's Soft Power: Buddha to Bollywood*.

Note:

(1-1): Note: Minor Rock Edict No. 1 (conflated versions)

English translation

From Suvarnagiri, on the order of His Highness the Prince, and the officers: good health to the officers of Isila who are to be instructed thus:

Thus speaks the Beloved of the Gods, Asoka:

I have been a Buddhist layman (*Upasaka*)/a Buddha-Saka /a Saka for more than two and a half years, but for a year I did not make much progress. Now for more than a year I have drawn closer to the Order (*Sangha*) and have become more ardent. The gods, who in India up to this time did not associate with men, now mingle with them, and this is the result of my efforts.

Moreover, this is not something to be obtained only by the great, but it is also open to the humble, if they are earnest and they can even reach heaven easily.

This is the reason for this announcement that both humble and great should make progress and that the neighbouring peoples also should know that the progress is lasting,

And this investment will increase and increase abundantly, and increase to half as much again.

This matter must be inscribed here and elsewhere on the hills, and wherever there is a stone pillar it is to be engraved on that pillar. You must go out with this document throughout the length and breadth of your district.

This announcement has been proclaimed while on tour; 256 nights have been spent on tour.

– Adapted from Romilla Thapar, A translation of the Edicts of Ashoka)

(1-2): The translation of inscription (by Paranavitana) reads: "When King Devanampriya Priyadarsin had been anointed twenty years, he came himself and worshiped (this spot) because the Buddha Shakyamuni was born here. (He) both caused to be made a stone bearing a horse and caused a stone pillar to be set up, (in order to show) that the Blessed One was born here. (He) made the village of Lumbini free of taxes, and paying (only) an eighth share (of the produce)."

(1-3): The Lokottaravada was one of the early Buddhist schools. The 6th century CE Indian monk Paramartha wrote that 200 years after the parinirvaṇa of the Buddha, much of the Mahasaṃghika school moved north of Rajagriha, and were divided over whether the Mahayana teachings should be incorporated formally into their

Tripitaka. According to this account, they split into three groups based upon the relative manner and degree to which they accepted the authority of these Mahayana texts. According to Paramartha, the Lokottaravadins accepted the Mahayana *sutras* as the words of the Buddha (buddhavacana).

(1-4): The Anoma was a river in Majjhimadesa of ancient India. According to Buddhist tradition it was situated near Kapilavastu, and was crossed by Prince Siddhartha (along with his horse Kanthaka and charioteer Channa) where he renounced the world before becoming the Buddha by cutting off his hair, abandoning his royal dress and exchanging it for the robes of an ascetic. Alexander Cunningham identified it with the Aumi in Gorakhpur district of Uttar Pradesh, while A. C. L. Carlleyle states it is the Kudwa Nala, a small creek in the Basti district.

(1-5): *Pabbajja Sutta*: The Going Forth", by Thanissaro BhikkhuI.

I will describe the Going Forth,
how he, the One-with-Vision, went forth,
how he reasoned and chose the Going Forth.
"Household life is crowded,
a realm of dust,
while going forth
is the open air."
Seeing this, he went forth.
On going forth,
he avoided evil deeds in body.
Abandoning verbal misconduct,
he purified his livelihood.
Then he, the Buddha, went to Rajagaha,
the mountain fortress of the Magadhans,
and wandered for alms,
endowed with all the foremost marks.
King Bimbisara, standing in his palace, saw him,
and on seeing him, consummate in marks,

said: "Look at this one, sirs.
How handsome, stately, pure!
How consummate his demeanor!
Mindful, his eyes downcast,
looking only a plow-length before him,
as one who's not from a lowly lineage:
Send the royal messengers at once
to see where this monk will go."
They – the messengers dispatched –
followed behind him.
    "Where will this monk go?
    Where will his dwelling place be?"
As he went from house to house –
well-restrained, his sense-doors guarded,
    mindful, alert –
his bowl filled quickly.
Then he, the sage, completing his alms round,
left the city, headed for Mount Pandava.
    "That's where his dwelling will be."
Seeing him go to his dwelling place,
three messengers sat down,
while one returned to tell the king.
"That monk, your majesty,
on the flank of Pandava,
sits like a tiger, a bull,
a lion in a mountain cleft."
Hearing the messenger's words,
the noble warrior king
straight away went by royal coach,
out to Mount Pandava.
Going as far as the coach would go,
he got down, went up on foot,
and on arrival sat down.

Sitting there,
he exchanged courteous greetings,
then said:
"You are young, youthful,
in the first stage of youth,
endowed with the stature & colouring
    of a noble-warrior.
You would look glorious
    in the vanguard of an army,
    arrayed with an elephant squadron.
I offer you wealth : enjoy it.
I ask your birth : inform me."
"Straight ahead, your majesty,
by the foothills of the Himalayas,
is a country consummate
in energy & wealth,
inhabited by Kosalans:
    Solar by clan,
    Sakyans by birth.
From that lineage I have gone forth,
but not in search of sensual pleasures.
Seeing the danger in sensual pleasures
– and renunciation as rest –
            I go to strive.
    That's where my heart delights."

Note 2-1: (Gandhari –Gandhari was an Indo-Aryan Prakrit language found mainly in texts dated between the 3rd century BCE and 4th century CE in the region of Gandhara, located in the northwestern Indian subcontinent. The language was heavily used by the former Buddhist cultures of Central Asia and has been found as far away as eastern China, in inscriptions at Luoyang and Anyang.)

Note 2-2: Agama : In Buddhism, the term agama is used to refer to a collection of discourses (Sanskrit: *sutra*; Pali: *sutta*) of the early Buddhist schools, which were preserved primarily in Chinese translation, with substantial material also surviving in Prakrit/ Sanskrit and lesser but still significant amounts surviving

Note 2–3: This file is made available under the Creative Commons CC0 1. 0 Universal Public Domain Dedication.

The person who associated a work with this deed has dedicated the work to the public domain by waiving all of their rights to the work worldwide under copyright law, including all related and neighbouring rights, to the extent allowed by law. You can copy, modify, distribute and perform the work, even for commercial purposes, all without asking permission.

Note 4-1: Kalashoka or Kakavarna was the son and successor of Shishunaga, the founder of the Shishunaga dynasty of the Magadha Empire in the present day northern India. He divided his kingdom between his ten sons and crowned his ninth son, Nandivardhana as the king of Magadha.

4 (a) Patimokkha: it is *sutra* per excellence, a short statement of all the rules of the order which is recited on every Uposatha day. It was the day of the full moon. The members of the order resident in any one district are to meet together to hear the statement of this statement of the rules read.

Nikayas means collections.

Note 7-1: Sankhara or saṁskara is a term figuring prominently in Buddhism. The word means 'formations' or 'that which has been put together' and 'that which puts together'.

In English translations it is in the first sense of the word 'conditioned things,' 'determinations, 'fabrications and 'formations' (or, particularly when referring to mental processes, 'volitional formations'. In the second (active) sense of the word, sankhara refers to *karma* (sankhara-khandha) that leads to conditioned arising, dependent origination.

Sankhara is a Pali word that is cognate with the Sanskrit word samskara. The latter word is not a Vedic Sanskrit term, but found extensively in classical and epic era Sanskrit in all Indian philosophies.

INDEX